Ride into Adventure: Exciting Equestrian Tales

Francisco .N Chavez

All rights reserved. Copyright © 2023 Francisco .N Chavez

Funny helpful tips:

Practice mutual understanding; it's the key to harmony.

Stay persistent; perseverance often differentiates dreams achieved from those abandoned.

Ride into Adventure: Exciting Equestrian Tales : Experience Heart-Pumping Horse Stories: A Collection of Thrilling Equestrian Adventures.

Life advices:

Cultivate a sense of wonder; it keeps the spirit young and vibrant.

Stay solution-focused; problems are inevitable, but solutions drive progress.

Introduction

Embarking on the captivating journey of horseback riding opens a gateway to a world where the majestic partnership between human and horse takes center stage. This guide, tailored for beginners, unveils the fundamentals of understanding these remarkable creatures and delves into the artistry of riding.

The opening chapters gracefully introduce the basics of horses, laying the groundwork for a profound connection. From the diverse riding styles that showcase the elegance of equine movement to an exploration of various horse breeds, riders gain insight into the dynamic world of equestrianism.

Preparation is key, and this guide meticulously walks beginners through the steps of getting ready for a ride. From saddling up to understanding essential safety measures, the importance of a secure and enjoyable riding experience is emphasized.

Safety takes precedence as riders venture into the heart of their equestrian adventure. The "Safe Riding" section provides invaluable guidelines to ensure both rider and horse navigate the journey with confidence and security. Understanding the nuances of gaits, coupled with effective exercising and training techniques, sets the stage for a harmonious partnership.

For those with aspirations to leap into more advanced riding techniques, the section on jumping unveils the thrill and precision of this captivating discipline. From the basics to more intricate maneuvers, riders are guided through the exhilarating world of jumping.

As the ride concludes, riders are led through essential post-riding practices. Caring for the horse and equipment ensures the well-being of the four-legged partner, fostering a bond built on trust and respect.

Beyond the saddle, this guide extends into the realm of equestrian etiquette and games. Unveiling the unspoken rules of the horse world and introducing engaging games, riders discover the social and playful dimensions of the equestrian community.

In the pages of this book, the art, science, and joy of riding converge. Whether you're a novice seeking the thrill of the first ride or an aspiring equestrian with dreams of mastering advanced techniques, this guide is your passport to a world where the rhythmic beat of hooves echoes the shared language between rider and horse. Saddle up, feel the wind in your hair, and let the journey begin.

Contents

Chapter 1 – Understanding Horse Basics 1

    Mind 3

    Sight 5

    Hearing 6

    Smell 8

    Touch 10

    Body Language 12

    - Being Afraid 13
    - Being Attentive 13
    - Being Hostile and Feisty 14
    - Being Placid and Peaceful 14
    - Whinnying 14
    - Nicker 14
    - Blow 14
    - Snort 15
    - Squeal 15

    Movement 16

    The Anatomy of a Horse 16

    - Bull Neck 19
    - Ewe Neck 19
    - Forelegs 20
    - Hind Legs 20
    - Pasterns 20

    What it takes to own a horse 20

    Should you buy a horse? 20

- Hard Work 21
- Huge Responsibility 21
- Finance 22

Total Costs 22
- Purchase 22
- Equipment 24
- Board 24
- Bedding 26
- Feed and Supplements 26
- Veterinary Care 28
- Hooves and Shoes 28
- Insurance 29
- Riding Lessons 30
- Show Expenditure 30

Chapter 2 - Riding styles and Horse Breeds 33

Western Saddles 33
English Saddles 36
Bits and Bridles 39
Different bridle styles 41
Saddle Fitting 43
Different Breeds of Horses 45
Breeds 47
1. Appaloosa 47
2. Arabian 49
3. Miniature 51
1. Morgan 53
2. Paint Horse 55
3. Quarter Horse 58

    4.   Saddlebred 59
    5.   Tennessee Walking Horse 61
    6.   Thoroughbred 62
  Popular Pony Breeds 64
    1.   Shetland 64
    2.   Welsh 66
    3.   Connemara 67
    4.   Pony of the Americas 68
  Warmbloods 70
    1.   Hanoverian 72
    2.   Trakehner 73

Chapter 3 – Getting Ready for Your Ride 94

  Losing a pound or two 95
  Getting on and off 95
  Energy 96
  Aerobic exercise and endurance 96
  Strength 96
  Arms 97
  Legs 97
  Abdomen 98
  Flexibility 98
  It's all in mind 98
  Being the leader 98
  Fear 99
  Time for Lessons 100
  Finding the most suitable stable 100
  What you need for horseback riding 102
  Grooming 104

- Leg Wrapping and its purpose 106
- Uses of horse leg 108
- Rear leg wraps 109
- Front leg wraps 109
- Brushing 109
- Overreaching 109
- Leg wraps provide tendon support 110
- Should horses wear leg wraps when being transported? 110
- Types of leg wraps 111
- Longeing/Lungeing 111
- Bridles and Saddles 113
- How to put on a bridle 116
- How to put on a saddle 117

Chapter 4 – Safe Riding 119
- Safety Clothing 119
- Riding Hat 122
- Body Protectors 123
- Jewelry 123
- Clothes not to wear when riding 123
- Spooking 125
- Bucking 126
- Rearing 127
- Running Away 129
- Backing Up 129

Chapter 5 - Ride On 131
- Prepare to Mount 131
- Where to Mount 131
- Getting on 132

Prepare to mount 132
Holding the reins and cues 133
Rein cues 134
Natural Aids 135
Artificial Aids 139
- Crop 142
- Fly Whisk 143
- Dressage 143
- Quirt 143

Chapter 6 - Gaits, Exercising and Training 144
Western cues 146
English cues 146
The walk-in Western horseback riding 146
The walk-in Hunt seat 147
The Dressage Walk 148
Trotting 149
Diagonals and Posting 151
Cantering 153
Galloping 157
Backing up 159
Transitions 161
Exercise & Training Regimes 161
Gait Transitions 163
Patterns 163
1. Figure of 8 165
2. Spirals 165
3. Serpentine 166
4. Simple Serpentine 167

- 5. Volte and Reverse 167
- 6. Leg Yield – (Side pass in western) 168

Chapter 7 – Jumping 172
- Different types of jumping 173
- Jumping in an Arena 174
- Showjumping 174
- Hunters 176
- Cross-country jumping 178
- Types of fences 180
- Cross rail's/Cross Pole 181
- Verticals 182
- Oxers 184
- Walls 185
- The Jumping Process 188
- The 2-point position 188
- Time to Jump 189
- Multiple jumps 191
- Grid 192
- Keep inline 192
- On Course 193
- Jumping Issues 193
  - Hurrying 194
  - Running away 194
  - Refusing 195

Chapter 8 – When you finish your ride 197
- Dismounting 197
- Untacking your horse 198
- Cool your horse down 199

    Grooming after riding 200
Chapter 9 - Equestrian Etiquette and Games 202
    Red Ribbon 202
    Slow and Steady 204
    Communication is Key 205
    There is no need to Shout 206
    Keep Your Distance 206
    Approach with Caution 208
    Left Shoulder to Shoulder 209
    Prepare for Trail Riding 210
    Time for a Drink 211
    Help 212
    Time for Games 213
    Simon Says 215
    Magazine Race 215
    Red Light, Green Light 216
    Ride-a-Buck 217
    Treasure Trail 217
    Ride and Tie 217
Conclusion 219

Chapter 1 – Understanding Horse Basics

There are various reasons why people decide to take up horseback riding; however, the basics remain the same. In this chapter, we will look at the anatomy of a horse, its senses, mind, and body language, then finish with what it takes to own a horse. Before you get on a horse for the first time, there are many facts that you need to understand. Riding cannot compare to any other sport where your physical fitness determines success. Horseback riding is about how well you can develop your strength, coordination, and reactions, and whilst you have a partner in the horse, it is different from partnering with a golf club or hockey stick as the horse has a mind of its own! Success is measured by how well you get on as a team, and the better physical shape you are both in, the more you will succeed.

By being in control and truly understanding that a horse will be faster and stronger than you are, the first point you need to understand and how you can overcome these strengths is to understand the limitations the horse has, understanding the horse's body, how its brain works, and what makes it see you in total control.

Horses differ from humans as they cannot reason, and therefore, most of their training is a set of controlled actions which become habits. Whereas we can take in numerous senses, figure things out and plan, then react reasonably. Horses do not possess this capacity; therefore, the quicker you understand this, the easier it will be for you to handle a horse and know why it reacts in the way it does.

To become the best rider, you need to understand that horses do not chase other animals to eat or kill. Horses have the "flight or fight" instinct; more opt for flight, although some will stand their ground and fight. Whatever challenges a horse, such as a bit of paper blowing in the wind or a loud noise, will see the horse shy away from what they do not trust or understand.

As a rider, it is essential to understand that you are sitting on the most vulnerable part of a horse, its back. Whenever a lion chases a zebra, it will usually jump at the zebra's back, and therefore, when you are sitting on a horse's back, this can make them nervous. You must be constantly aware of this, and therefore you need to sit as still as possible and avoid making any movement that will make the horse fear you in its back.

Horses are herd animals, and therefore they want to be with other horses or a trusted owner/rider. Over the years, horses have found safety in numbers, and when they are together, there is more likelihood of at least one seeing a predator approaching. Don't be fooled because not all horses will get along; in fact, there is always a pecking order; one horse will emerge as the leader, and some horses are far more dominant than others, and there are also horses that are happier on their own.

When a human enters a horse's life, the instinct to follow a leader is beneficial. If you can influence your leadership over a horse from the beginning, you will find that you can control the horse straight away. It is ideal to gain the respect of a horse from day one; failure to do so will see the horse taking charge, and you will have a constant battle on your hands.

A horse's senses do not equate to those of a human; horses are prey animals, humans are predators. Both senses are used similarly but used in very different ways and processed differently in their brains. We are now going to look at the senses individually:

Mind

There are people that think horses are dumb, however, this statement could not be further from the truth. After all, horses have been around for millions of years, so they cannot be stupid, or they could never have stayed alive for long enough to still be a populated breed of animal today.

Horses' bodies are also amazing as they are designed for agility, speed, and survival. Horses can run fast, spin around on a dime and react physically at speed to the tiniest of sounds. If you want to ride a horse, you need to understand all of their abilities in depth.

As a rider, you need to be able to communicate with your horse. Horses do not view the world in the way that we do. Computers, mobile phones are not part of their world, it is hay, mud, and other horses that make up their world. Learning to see the world from your horse's perspective will make you a far better rider and make your entire riding experience far more enjoyable. The equine body and mind are at your fingertips if you know how to use them.

Sight

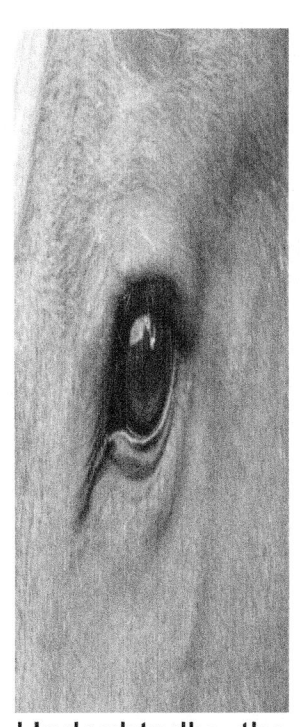

Undoubtedly the most important sense to a horse is its sight. Horses' eyes are on the side of their narrow, long face, and although horses have panoramic vision and can see almost 180 degrees on either side, they do possess a blind spot directly in front of them and behind them. Their forward vision is binocular to see in front of them up. Horses can see about one foot to the front of their head. There is a general belief that horses can see for hundreds of yards and may differentiate colors to a certain degree. Horses' night vision is far better than humans.

Hearing

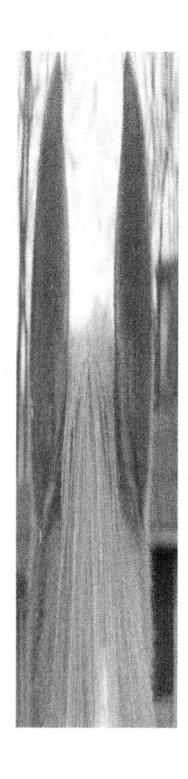

Horses have far better hearing than humans which you would expect from an animal that may have to get away from predators.

Horses' ears are conical in shape, and horses use their ears to channel sound into their ear canal. Horses can move their ears to the front and rear of their head and move them independently. Unlike humans, horses can process sound from both of their ears, with their brains programmed to take in the different sounds whilst they are either standing still or eating and determine whether they should be alerted. It is vital to remember that horses can get spooked from the slightest thing, so you should always be ready to reassure them that everything is ok. If your body tenses suddenly, the horse will be aware and could stop abruptly, run off, or even jump sideways.

Smell

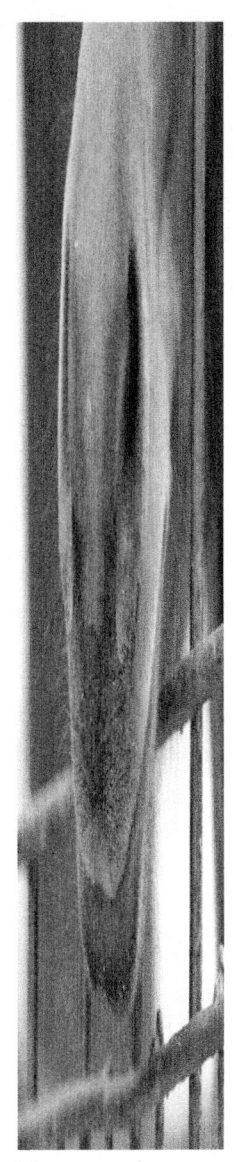

Horses have a far better sense of smell than humans.

Not only can they smell other animals around them, but they can also use their sense of smell to check out other horses. You may have noticed that horse's approach everyone with their nose, and this is how they can determine whether someone or something is friendly or not. You should always approach a horse that you do not know with the back of your hand in a slow gesture; at this point, the horse will sniff you and determine whether it is safe to be around you or not. Letting the horse smell you will put it at ease about you, failure to do this and the horse will probably flee because it cannot trust you.

Touch

Horses have thick skin, but not like you think because they can feel a fly land on them. Due to their well-created nerve endings, they can handle even the lightest of touches from other horses and humans alike. Be sure to watch when two horses meet, as they will touch each other with their noses and rub up against each other.

The sense of touch can be used by riders to their advantage when around a horse by gently rubbing it, patting the neck, and other areas. Horses particularly like to be petted around their ears and in between their eyes on their face. The key is to be slow and gentle,

and you will find that once the horse is used to you, it will lower its head, which is a sign that the horse trusts you and feels at ease with your actions.

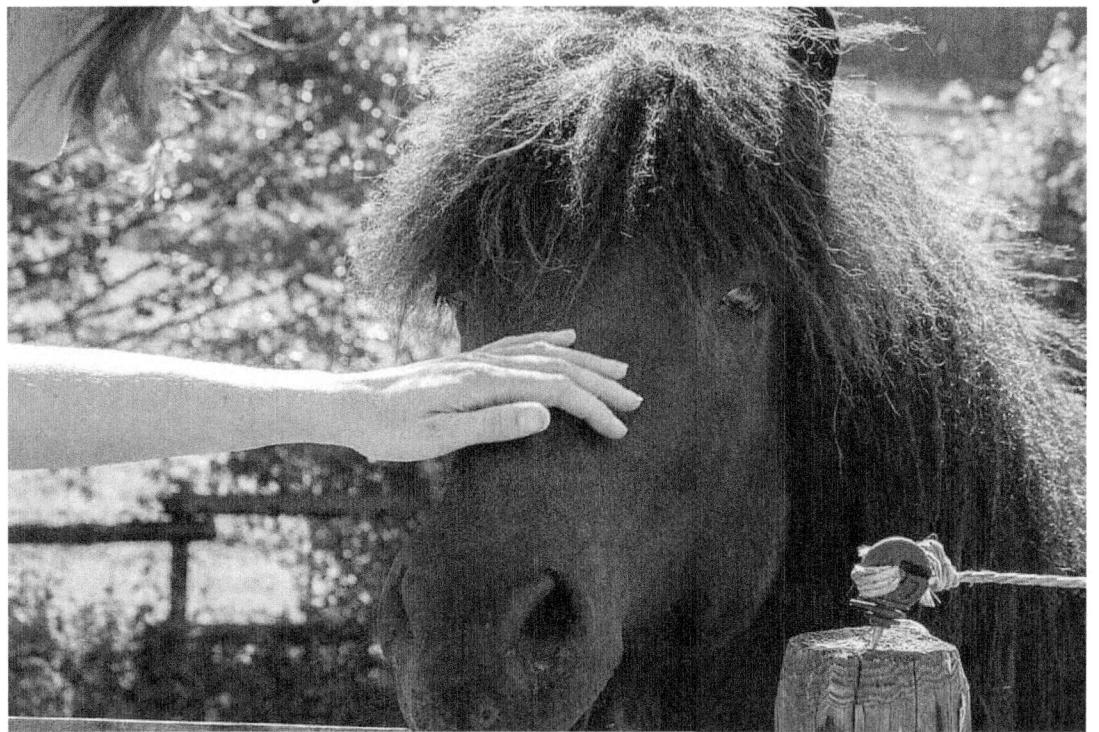

Body Language

Horses use body language every day, and they can also pick up on your body language as sociable animals' horses talk in many ways. You need to be able to decipher the primary body language a horse exhibits. One of the first signs of body language your parents have told you about horses is that they are angry when their ears lie flat back. Their laid-back ears may also come with plenty of teeth, depending on how angry they are.

As a horse owner, there are a plethora of other facial differences that you need to understand, such as:

- Being Afraid

When horses are scared, both of their ears will point towards what is scaring them; however, they could also stand with their head held high before turning tail and bolting! You may also notice their neck muscles tensing and nostrils flaring.

- Being Attentive

Many horses will naturally stand with their heads held high and ears pointing forwards. Rather than being scared, they may be happy with their surroundings.

- Being Hostile and Feisty

When a horse adopts the classic ears flat back looking menacing, the chances are that they are planning their next move, and this will either involve hooves or teeth!

- Being Placid and Peaceful

When a horse is relaxed, you will immediately be able to tell as their head will be at an average height, their eyelids may sag a little, their ears may drop to the side, and their bottom lip may be loose. It is this expression that you will probably see when they fall asleep or have a relaxing groom.

Every horse will have their variations on the gestures above, and as you spend more time with them, you will soon grasp their gestures.

The body language of a horse can also be vocal such as:

- Whinnying

Whinnying is how a horse lets you know they are there, and it is their way of saying, "Don't forget I am here!" They will also whinny when they are lonely.

- Nicker

When a horse nickers, it is a low nasal sound that omits from a closed mouth. This is how a horse will usually greet their owners and other horses. It is a warm and kind sound.

- Blow

There are several ways that a horse can blow, and you can

compare it with a human sighing; horses blow when you ask them to do something that they do not want to. They also blow as a warning or when they are curious about something new. Some horses blow when they are relaxed as well.

- Snort

Horses snort, which is the equivalent of a harsh blow, horses snort in disapproval, and when they meet other horses, the snort can also be aggressive and assertive.

- Squeal

When a horse squeals, it sounds worse than it is and is used to assert its authority. Although it sounds aggressive, there is very little aggression; it is more of curiosity.

Movement

You must understand how quickly horses can move, and not only are they fast, but they are also a considerable force with legs that can move faster than you may realize. Not only can they kick with their hind legs, but they can also itch their ears with their back hooves.

Horses have large, firm heads, shoulders, and necks, so much so that they could easily knock you off your feet with a simple movement. Horses can also swing around and turn incredibly quickly; therefore, if you were to find yourself at the side of a horse that decided to move or flee, you will feel the full force of their body and believe me, you are no match for that.

Horses can move incredibly quickly, and if you go up behind them and scare them, they will either kick out with their hind legs or flee. Therefore, you should always approach a horse from the front, and should you have something the horse is unsure about, they may rear or back away quickly. If you have the horse on a lead rein, do not attempt to stop their movement backward because this could excite them further, resulting in a terrible accident or, worse still, the horse landing on its back.

The Anatomy of a Horse

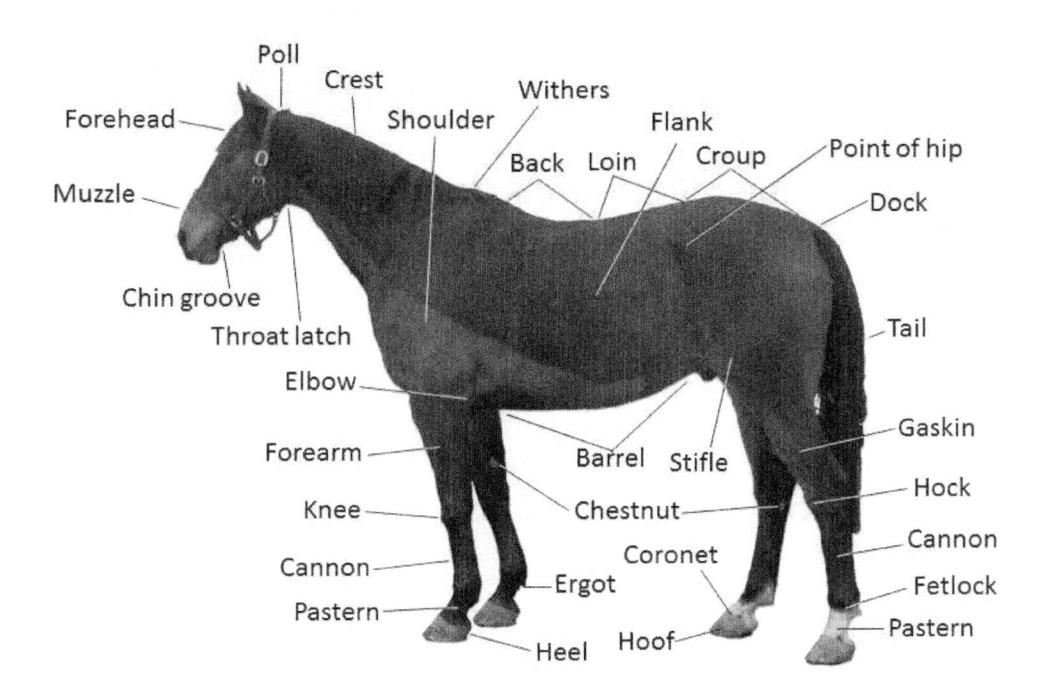

Diagram of horse anatomy with labels: Poll, Crest, Withers, Flank, Forehead, Shoulder, Croup, Point of hip, Back, Loin, Muzzle, Dock, Chin groove, Throat latch, Tail, Elbow, Forearm, Barrel, Stifle, Gaskin, Knee, Chestnut, Hock, Cannon, Coronet, Cannon, Ergot, Fetlock, Pastern, Heel, Hoof, Pastern.

If you plan to own or spend a lot of time with horses, you need to learn as many parts of the horse as possible. This will be particularly helpful should the horse get injured because you will know what to tell the vet. Even if you are riding, there are certain areas of the horse that you should know as this will assist when you are being taught by a riding instructor or being self-taught from a book.

On a horse's head, the most critical areas are the mouth, throatlatch, and poll. The poll is the space between the horse's ears and is incredibly sensitive, so much that should a horse take a hard hit to the poll, they could die; therefore, it is vital that you are careful of this area and never hit the horse with anything between its ears. The throatlatch is the connector with the horse's neck and head, where the bridle buckles up. The mouth has various parts you can get acquainted with, but most important is the area without the teeth; this is the bars of the mouth and where the bit rests within the horse's mouth.

Moving onwards, at the top of a horse's neck is the crest, and at the bottom are the withers. The crest and the withers vary in size, and each horse and breed will be different. The withers are very important as this is how you fit the saddle and where the saddle pad and saddle rest. When you look at a horse, it is obvious their back is between the withers and the loins, which you can locate at the flanks. This connects the horse's belly to its hindquarters. The high point of the hindquarters is the croup and extends to the base of the tail, the dock. Moving down from the hindquarters, you have the part that sticks out at the back of the leg called the hock; down from this, you will find the cannon, ankle, and pastern. The front legs start with the shoulder at the top, connecting the leg to the forearm, followed by the knee, cannon, and fetlock.

These parts of the horse are what you need to know as an owner and or rider, as this is how you can identify whether a horse has good conformation. Conformation denotes how the horse moves, and there are several conformation faults that you need to be aware of before buying a horse, such as:

- Bull Neck

A bull often has this type of neck hence the name, and on a horse, it appears as an abnormally large neck that blends into the shoulder with no kind of definition. You should be careful not to confuse a bull neck with a large crest which is part of the correct makeup of Lipizzaner and Andalusian horses.

- Ewe Neck

Horses with an ewe neck have a usually thin odd-shaped neck that appears arched and very thin towards the top of the head.

- Forelegs

You can find many flaws on a horse's front legs, including toes that turn out or in; the feet can appear too close together on a narrow base which can make the horse appear to have bowed legs; alternatively, the feet can be too far apart with the knees together.

- Hind Legs

In the same way as the front legs, the hind legs can share the same defects, easy to spot in the hocks.

- Pasterns

Having issues in the pasterns can lead to lameness; if the pasterns are too upright, the horse will look as if it is digging into the ground as it moves, whereas a horse with long pasterns can appear to be slapping the ground when it moves.

What it takes to own a horse

Most people who start horseback riding inevitably want a horse before long. Once the horseback riding bug has bitten you, you can never shift it! However, owning a horse is expensive, but it requires a lot of time, and you need to be 100% committed, so it is not a decision to be taken lightly.

Should you buy a horse?

It is wonderful to own a horse as you can ride whenever you want, but the reality can be different from what you think, and therefore you need to be confident that you are able to, before taking this huge step. The following should help you to decide whether you are ready to make such a big commitment.

- Hard Work

Horses are hard work, and it is not all about having fun and riding whenever you want. If your horse has a stable at your home, you will have to feed him or her, clean out the stable and groom your horse. Whilst mucking out the stable and clearing muck from the field is not the most glamorous of jobs, it is essential and must be done.

- Huge Responsibility

Your horse will be dependent on you for whatever they need, such as food, water, companionship, and exercise, and your horse must be your main priority. No longer can jet off to the sun on a whim or go out without arranging horse care. Horses can live to be over 30 years old, so you are signing up for a long time of cold winters where you will have to brave arctic conditions because your horse needs you.

- Finance

Owning a horse does not come cheap, with the initial outlay of the horse being the first of many costs that you need to factor. Horses need food, visits from the farrier, veterinary care, and if you are keeping the horse at home, there is the upkeep to the stable and or field shelter to consider. If you cannot keep your horse at home, you then need to think about the costs to keep your horse in someone else's yard.

Horse ownership is expensive and not something you should take on lightly. Horses have specific needs and are magnificent animals that deserve to be looked after by people that genuinely care about them.

Total Costs

Before you decide to buy a horse, you need to work out precisely what you can spend as horses are expensive to purchase and costly to keep. You can expect to pay out the following when owning your horse:

- Purchase

The amount you can spend on a horse will depend on many factors, including the horse's age, the level of schooling they are at, and whether you want to show them. The prices of horses do tend to vary depending on where you live; however, you should be prepared to pay a minimum of $1,500.00 for the pleasure of purchasing a horse, and this will be considerably more if you intend on showing your horse.

- Equipment

The next cost to factor in is the equipment and supplies that you need, which at the least will include tack (saddle and bridle), saddle pad, grooming brushes, rugs, and a halter. Then there is the clothing you will need, and if you plan to keep the horse at home and do not have the shelter or stables, you need to factor in the costs for these, which can be substantially dependent on what you need to do.

- Board

If you cannot keep your horse at home, you need to find somewhere to keep it, which means you must pay for the board, a field or paddock, and bedding. This establishment will usually include building maintenance and food but may or may not include bedding.

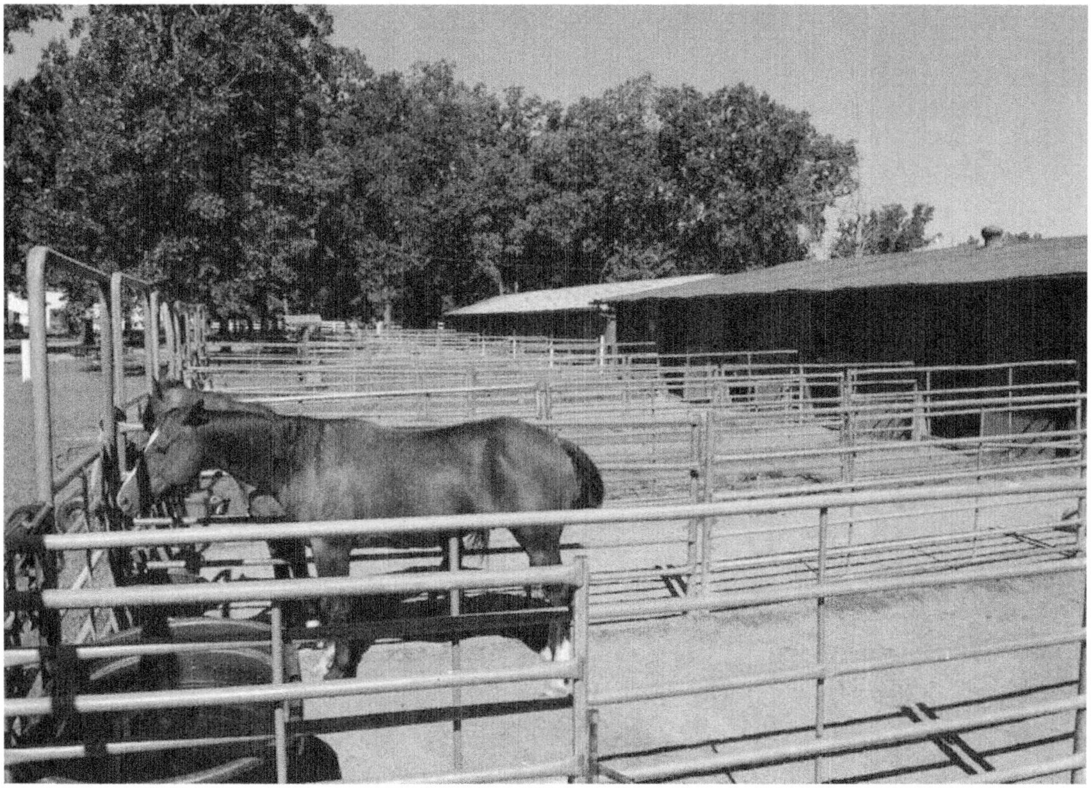

- Bedding

Regardless of where your horse lives, it will need bedding, and whilst there are different types of bedding, you will need to keep it clean and freshen it up every day.

- Feed and Supplements

Horses need to eat, and as well as pasture and hay, they

require food such as pony nuts, and you should also think about other costs to be incurred in a situation where your horse has any special dietary requirements. There are many supplements that you can feed a horse to keep its joints supple, curb its attitude, and so on. If you are planning to use supplements, you must also include these in your costs.

- Veterinary Care

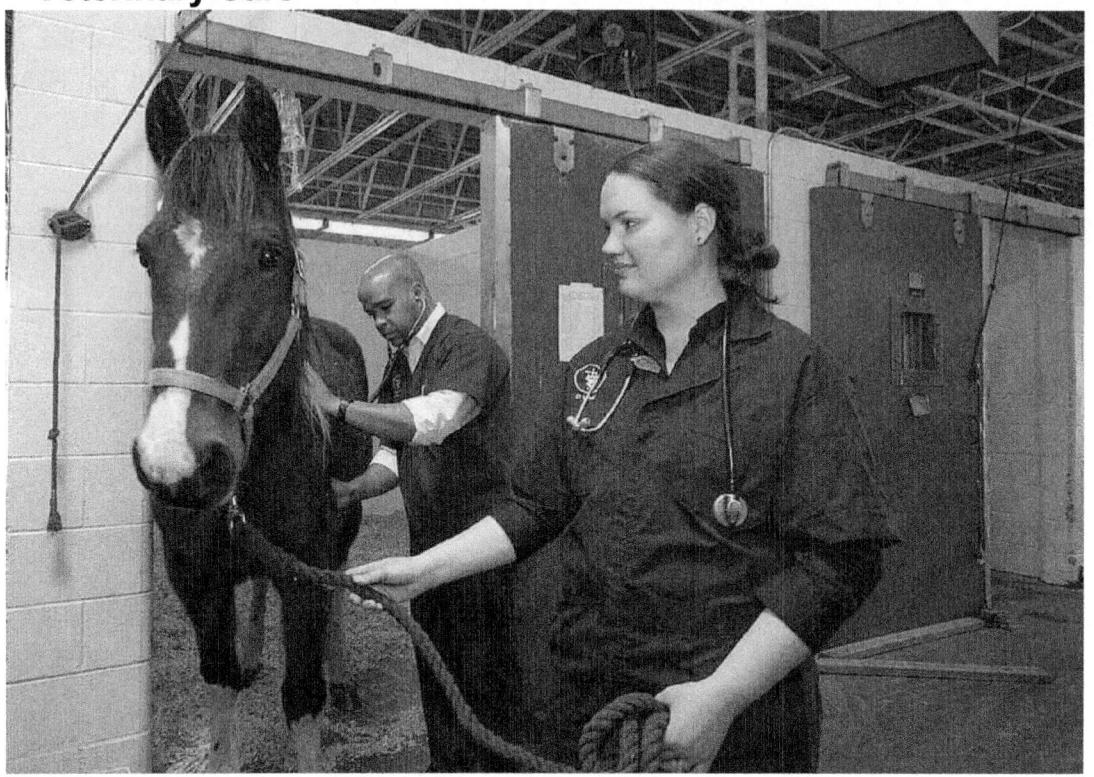

Horses require preventative veterinary care, including deworming and vaccinating several times a year. They also need to have their teeth rasped a minimum of twice a year. Other veterinary costs to think about is if your horse gets sick and they do, you may need to call out the vet. Whilst the horse may have a minor illness, you need to be cautious as something significant may require surgery, and vet bills can be costly and rise quickly if your horse has a severe condition that requires urgent treatment.

- Hooves and Shoes

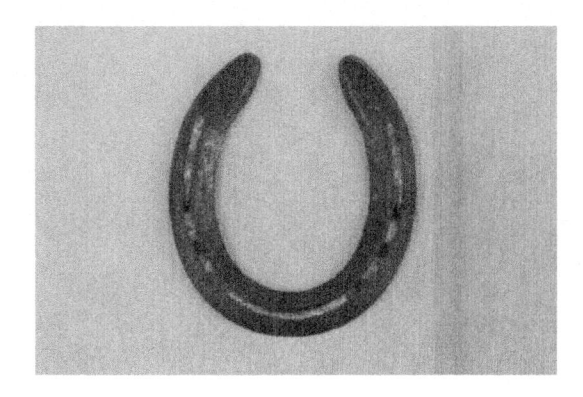

of outgoings.

If your horse wears shoes, they will need these changed at least once every eight weeks. Shoeless horses will also need to have their feet trimmed by the farrier regularly.

- **Insurance**

If you choose to insure your horse against veterinary bills, loss of use, and liability coverage, you must add the cost of the premiums to your list

- **Riding Lessons**

If you have recently started riding, you will still require lessons from a qualified instructor; this is a must if you intend to show your horse. You must remember to add these costs to your outgoings.

- **Show Expenditure**

If you are going to show your horse, you will need to purchase show clothes; then there is the tack, entry fee, and transportation.

Once you have calculated the total costs, you will see whether horse ownership fits your budget. However, you can enjoy using a horse without the initial outlay or bills by loaning a horse. There are many opportunities to lend a horse, meaning you get to ride and look after a horse for a fraction of the cost. Technically you are sharing the cost of the horse with its owner, and you are getting to ride and take care of it. Although this is an excellent idea if you cannot afford the total outlay, it is rather like renting a home, it will never be yours, and you have no way to recoup any of your costs.

Chapter 2 - Riding styles and Horse Breeds

When you start horseback riding, there are several riding styles that you can choose from. Every discipline has its unique style and competitive events that they are associated with. When selecting your horseback riding style, you need to think about what you want to achieve with your horse and what your horse can do.

If you are looking to spend your weekends trailing, your best choice would be to get yourself a well-cushioned western saddle that will make the whole experience as pleasurable as possible. If you want to jump, you must learn to ride English style and use an English saddle.

You may choose a specific discipline because it is popular where you live, and there is a good range of instructors and competitions that you can take part in. You will find that some styles are much more prevalent in different places of the country, for example, English riding (jumper, dressage, and hunter) in the North or Western riding in the West. We will have a more in-depth look at the various styles below.

Western Saddles

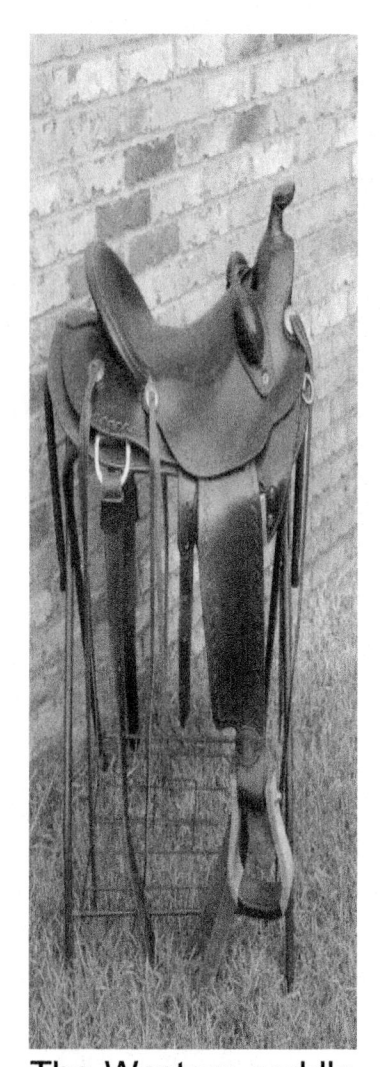

The Western saddle provides comfort and security, and therefore many horseback riders choose to learn this style of riding. The saddles are cushioned and large, which lends them, particularly to long rides. This type of saddle was designed by cowboys who sometimes spent days horseback riding and needed comfort.

There are many varieties of Western saddles, which are designed to suit many specific riding styles and events, and designed for pleasure, roping, cutting, barrel racing, reining, and trail riding. Western saddles have their unique features, which depend on what style of riding they are designed for. The cutting saddle has a deep seat and large cantles to hold onto when the horse makes quick movements; the roping saddle has a large horn for dallying your rope. The barrel saddle is light and has less skirt, and if you want to ride Western for fun, you will probably choose the trail or pleasure saddle.

If your interest is Western horseback riding, many cowhands work with cattle and use Western saddles. Western saddles are a large part of cowboy heritage and not something that will fall from fashion; however, the most significant function of the Western saddle today is for horseback riding pleasure horses and Western show horses. There are many events that riders can take part in riding Western such as rodeos, trail riding, Western pleasure, cutting, roping, reining, and gymkhana. If you are planning to horseback ride for fun, you will probably use a comfortable Western saddle.

The breed of horse you will most commonly see in full Western tack includes the Quarter Horse; however, this breed has also crossed over into English and dressage. Appaloosas and the Paint are also large Western breeds. It is rare to see a Thoroughbred in a Western saddle, but many work in a Western saddle. The Tennessee Walking Horse and Missouri Fox Trotter are usually ridden in Western, and Arabian horses can use Western tack when they are shown. Because of this, special Western saddles have been developed for the shorter backs and petite bodies.

English Saddles

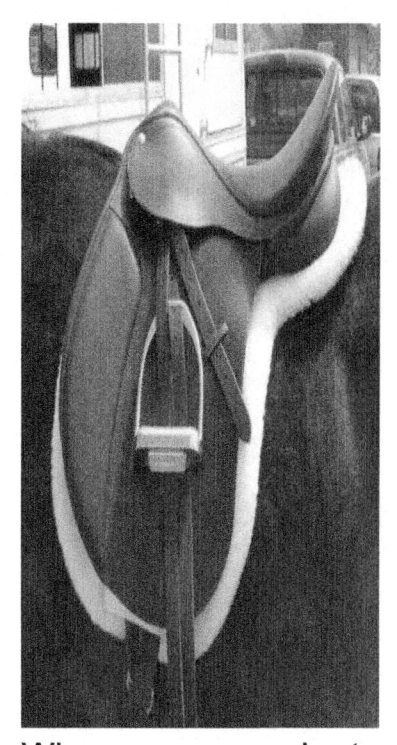

When compared to the Western saddle, the English is much lighter and smaller. The style of English horseback riding is often called a Hunt Seat, which references the traditional foxhunts that used to take place in England. The English saddle is simple with stirrup leathers and metal stirrups.

The English saddle does not give riders the security that the Western saddles do, and as the rider, you need to rely on your balance far more, but you do have closer contact with the horse and can feel the movements of the horse's shoulders and body. There are many different varieties of the English saddle which vary in the seat depth, breadth of the saddle twist, flap placement, such as the hunt seat saddle, dressage saddle, jumper saddle, hunt seat saddle, and the general-purpose saddle. The stirrup leathers are easily adjustable so that you can adjust the length and ensure that your weight is distributed evenly. This is vital as the English rider uses shorter stirrups than a Western rider would, particularly jumping.

In most English events, riders can use the general-purpose saddle, including jumping and sometimes dressage. More experienced riders could find the general-purpose saddle is not specific enough for their discipline of horseback riding and may choose to use a dressage saddle, showjumping saddle, hunt saddle, or saddle seat.

Bits and Bridles

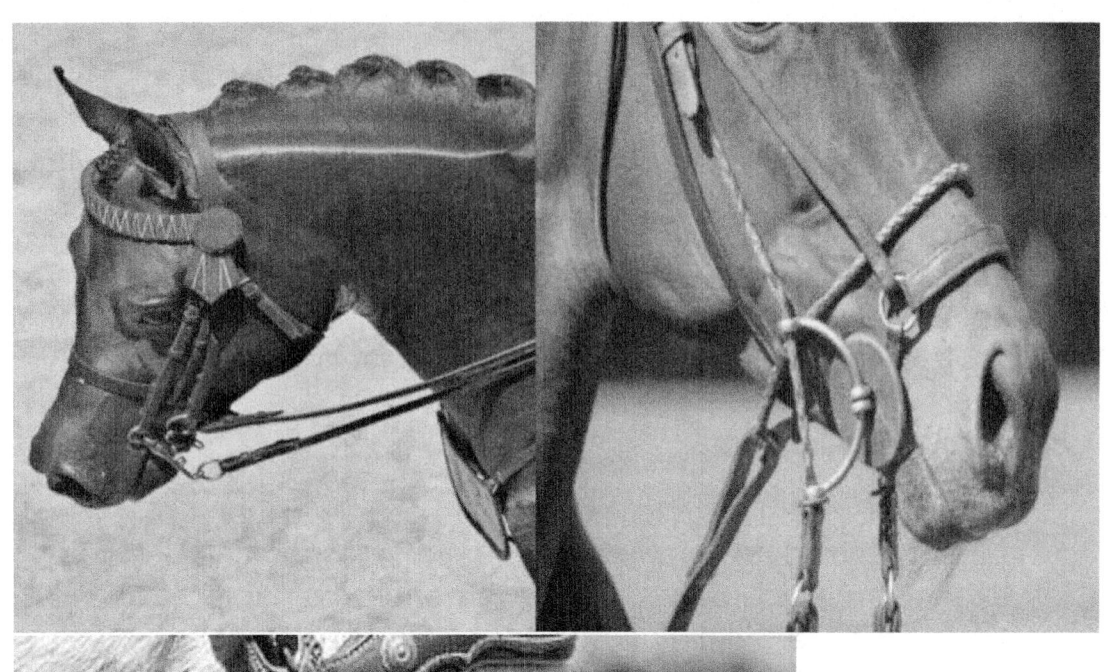

In the same way as the English saddle, certain types of bridle and bits are used for each discipline. The primary method of communication for a rider with their horse is the bit and bridle. The bit is held in place by the bridle, and it is the bit that encourages the horse to adopt the correct way to carry its head. The rider, in essence, sends signals through the bit and bridle through the specific pressure points horses have on their tongue, lips, and nose.

Different bridle styles

There are many different bridle styles, but these will all fit under the category of either Western or English. Typically, Western bridles have a simple leather headstall and may or may not have browbands or throat latches; some will also have some simple leather loops that fit around the horse's ears.

Traditionally a curb bit is used with Western horseback riding, although you can also use a snaffle bit. If using a curb bit, there will also be a curb chain. The curb bit has long bars that the reins are attached to. Many showy bridles are available and can be silver in color and complete with beading for competing in shows; these also vary in design and style.

English bridles also come in several different variations to match the various saddle types. The bridle typically has a single rein that is attached to a snaffle bit. The English bridle has a browband, throat latch, and cavesson (also known as the noseband).

English bits are made from various types of metal, with some of the best bits made from aluminum, but these can be hard to find. The aluminum bit is exceptionally light, and horses find them easy to carry in their mouths. Today, it is more common for bits to be made of copper and steel, with the copper being inlaid into the steel as this encourages the horses to salivate and keep what is known as a soft mouth. When you choose your bit for horseback riding, you must determine your horse's training level.

One of the most popular and safest bits is the snaffle as it is simple and gives you direct contact for turning your horse. The snaffle bit is made using a jointed steel bar with a large ring on either end where the cheek pieces and reins attach. There are different rings, and these can be O-rings, Egg-butt rings, or D-rings.

The double bridle is unique and used mainly in dressage and other show events. This predominantly English bit consists of a snaffle and curb bit. The double bridle gives the horse a collected and tucked head in appearance and features two reins. The pelham bit is also a combination of the snaffle and curb bit and is used predominantly for hunters, where the rider requires more control than they would get from a straight curb chain. The pelham bit has two sets of reins and a curb chain, and there are various rings on the bit to choose from and mainly used when hunting, jumping, or playing polo.

The curb bit consists of a single bar mouthpiece with a half-moon port in the center. There are variations with different port heights, and the breed associations have varied rules that regulate the port height if you are showing your horse. The port helps discourage the horse from getting its tongue over the bit, with the curb bit leveraging on the bars of the mouth.

Hackamores are a device that gives you control of a horse without having to use a bit in its mouth. There are Western and English versions of the hackamore, and they are mechanical and include metal shanks and a type of protective metal loop which goes over the bridge of the nose. The English hackamore uses a leather strap over the nose. You cannot use these bridles in competitions.

The Western bosal can also be referred to as a hackamore as it works in the same way. This bridle consists of a rawhide loop that goes around the horse's nose, and there are rope-style reins the rider can use to control their horse.

Saddle Fitting

If your saddle does not fit properly, you will not get very far, many horses have sore backs and will try all manner of things to stop you from riding them, and this is usually down to an ill-fitting saddle. A well-fitting saddle will not create any pressure points, rock, or pinch the horse's back. If there is a bald patch around the horse's withers, it usually indicates that the saddle is rubbing. The saddle tree must be the correct width and shape for the horse's back.

If the saddle is too wide, it will sit low on the withers and create pressure on the top of the withers. If the saddle is too narrow, it will pinch the withers' base, rub the hair off, and ride high in the front, causing the rider to get thrown back, creating pressure points to the back of the saddle. The saddle should be perfectly balanced, so you can maintain your balance regardless of how much the horse throws you about.

It is vital that the saddle also fits you, but it is far easier to fit a saddle to a rider than it is to a horse. I would encourage you to go to a tack shop and try out various saddles before trying it on a horse. Most saddles are measured in inches; however, ascertaining which size means trying a few out until you get the right fit.

When you check to see whether the saddle is the right fit for your horse, place it on its back without a saddle pad. The saddle should touch the right areas of your horse regardless of whether you are using a Western or English saddle. Once the rider is mounted, you should be able to fit two fingers between the saddle and the horse's withers. It would be best to run your hand over the back of the shoulder blade and under the front of the saddle to make sure that the saddle does not dig or pinch these areas; doing this will give the horse ample room for its spine and movement in their shoulders.

Saddle pads are used predominantly for the horse's comfort, and these vary and are dependent on the saddle you are using. The cushioning that the saddle pad provides allows for your weight to be evenly distributed along your horse's back, which helps the horse to carry your weight. However, you must be careful as using too much cushioning could unbalance your horse.

Different Breeds of Horses

Throughout the world, there are hundreds of horse breeds. Every breed has its unique qualities and has been bred for specific uses. While you can find most horse breeds in the US, several traditional popular, more common breeds exist. Some disciplines are more common in some areas than others; therefore, it stands to reason that some breeds will be more popular than others.

When you consider buying a horse, you will most likely purchase one of the more popular breeds as these are more readily available and suitable for a wide variation of budgets. If you want to show or compete in breed-specific classes or breed from your horse, you may want to investigate various options with breed-registered societies. Many horse breeds have qualities that breeders and horse owners have grown to love and appreciate.

There are a lot of people who successfully compete and show

horses that have no known pedigree. If you are not interested in competing or purchasing a breed-specific horse, you will find that your options are far broader. If you buy an unregistered breed, there are also many other competitions you can enter. The United States Equestrian Federation, the National Reining Horse Association, the United States Dressage Federation, and the National Cutting Horse Society do not require breeds to be registered to compete. There is also a rodeo and similar activities that you can take part in. In England, you also have plenty of options such as show jumping/hunter, dressage, and eventing competitions that will allow you to show regardless of breed and registration. There are numerous crossbreeds of popular breeds that make excellent show or weekend riding horses.

It would help if you also remembered that whilst most horses in the breeds will have similar personality traits, each horse is individual in the same way every person offers unique qualities. In the way that your upbringing through childhood has some bearing on the person you grow up to be, the way horses are treated as foals will affect the horses they become. An excellent example of this is the Shetland pony, notorious for its grumpy characteristics, but some are loving and adorable. Arabs are known to be highly strung, but some are excellent mounts and entirely trustworthy.

Breeds

Due to the number of breeds available to potential purchasers/used for riding lessons, I will concentrate on the more popular in both the United States and England.

1. **Appaloosa**

The Appaloosa is a well-known American breed and is a direct descendant of the Spanish Jennet horses that came to America in the 15th century. This is one of the most popular breeds that you will see competing in America and being a favorite amongst the equestrian fraternity. They are athletic, compact, strong horses that excel in Trail riding, endurance, Western stock classes, dressage and jumping, and being an excellent family horse.

Appaloosa's typically stand 14.2 to 16 hands and have five coats, including marble, snowflake, frost, leopard, and blanket. There are no registered grey or pinto Appaloosa's.

2. Arabian

The Arabian horse breed originated from the Bedouin tribes in the Arabian Peninsula and became popular in both America and England during the sixties. During the eighties, a glut of hot-blooded horses was bred to make them challenging to manage. Arabian horses were bred for show purposes. However, many became dangerous. Nowadays, the breed has settled down and is now an all-around breed that is good for various disciplines.

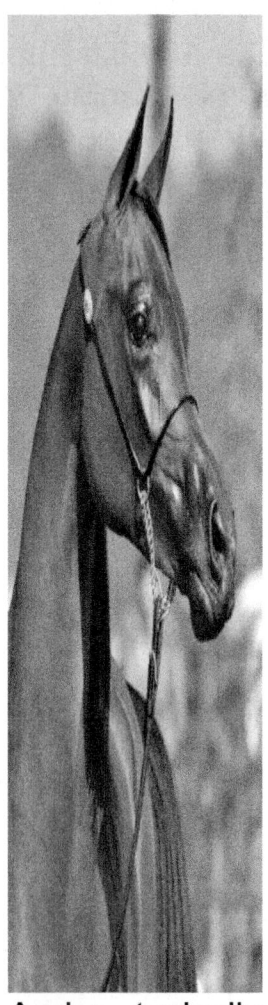

Arabs typically stand between 14.2 and 15

hands and are used for eventing, jumping, dressage, and endurance. The most common Arabs are black, grey, chestnut, bay, or roan.

3. **Miniature**

Although Miniature horse breeds are not ridden, they are hugely popular and incredibly versatile. The Miniature horse breed is tiny horses, not ponies, which have been stunted in growth by the harsh environments, including severe weather, rough terrain, and scarce food sources. Miniature horses were used in America to pull carts through the coal mines. The first miniature horses were developed in the 17th century in Europe and were bred as pets of nobility. Miniature horses are incredible as they have the same confirmation as a full-sized horse.

There are two height divisions of the Miniature horse recognized by the American Miniature Horse Association, these being the A division which stands under 34 inches, and the B division, which stands from 34 inches to 38 inches. Miniature horses are available in all colors and used for special events developed for their sizes, including halter, pleasure driving, and companions.

1. **Morgan**

Morgan horses originated in 1790 when Justin Morgan of Randolph, Vermont, took a yearling as payment for a debt, and the yearling Figure grew into a stunning stallion that was in huge demand as a stud and to this day, most Morgan horses can be traced back to his bloodline. The Morgan Stud has made considerable contributions to various breeds today and is a diverse and versatile breed.

Morgan horses stand from 14 to 15.2 and are usually black, chestnut, brown, bay, grey, cream, palomino, buckskin, and dun. The Morgan horse excels in dressage, jumping, driving, cattle cutting, cross country, endurance, and therapeutic riding. The breed is an excellent choice for children.

2. Paint Horse

Paints are often misdescribed as pintos; however, you must know the difference between all colored horses. The Paint Horse is an actual breed, whereas pinto is a color. This means that many Paints are pintos, but not all pintos are Paints. The Paint breed is the result of crossing many Quarter horses. The result is a stock-type horse that does not qualify for registration with the American Quarter Horse Association due to their white markings, even though many are predominantly Quarter Horse bred.

The breed was developed in the 1960s when Paint Horse enthusiasts started to breed and promote the horses as an individual breed. Paint horses have three coat markings which include:
- Tobiano has a white base with dark-colored patches on the top

- Overo, which are mainly a dark-colored base with white marking on top, what is interesting is that the markings on some Paints are jagged
- Tovero is a horse that is a combination of the Tobiano and Overo hence the name

The Paint horses stand from 15 – 16 hands in height, and several colors come within their markings, including bay, black, palomino, chestnut, roan, grey, buckskin, and black. The Paint horses are ideal for competing in Western stock classes, jumping, dressage, flat racing, trail riding, English classes, ranch work, and pleasure horses.

3. Quarter Horse

The most popular breed in the world is the American Quarter Horse. The number of registered Quarter horses stands at about 4 million, and there are affiliated registries in various countries. Due to the versatility of the Quarter horse, they are used to compete in English, Western, and pleasure driving and have recently become a popular choice with dressage riders.

There are rules with this breed on how much white they have and the white color's area, but you will come across Quarter horses in every color except for pinto. Quarter horses stand between 14 – 16 hands and are used for various events such as Western, English, jumping, driving, trail riding, flat racing, dressage, and pleasure riding.

4. Saddlebred

The Saddlebred has been developed from several breeds, including the Morgan, Narragansett Pacers, and Spanish horses. The horse derives from Kentucky and is a horse to cover long distances with a rider effortlessly. Famous for the stepping pace, known as the rack, as well as walk, trot, and canter, which are also very animated. There are three-gait and five-gait Saddlebreds; the five-gait horse performs the usual basic gaits and the stepping pace and rack, whereas the three-gait horses perform the three basic gaits. The Saddlebred tends to carry its head high and move in a collected way, it has a lean body, and they are often driven or ridden in both Western and English disciplines.

Saddlebred horses' range in height from 15 – 17 hands and most commonly are black, chestnut, bay, sorrel, brown, grey, and pinto. Saddlebreds excel in English driving classes as well as for pleasure. Recently this breed has begun to do well in jumping and dressage.

Although Standardbreds are best known for their adept harness racing skills, they also make great riding companions. The breed originated early in American history and was developed specifically for harness racing. The Standardbred tend to perform at a trot and can move at incredible speeds, some trot at almost 30 miles an hour. The pace is identifiable easily as the horse's legs move in unison, one side then the other. Closely related to the Thoroughbred and when they can no longer race, they compete at shows in both western and English events.

The Standardbred typically stands between 15 – 16 hands and are black, brown, chestnut, bay, and grey. As well as harness racing, Standardbreds also fare well in Western and English Classes and as a pleasure ride.

5.   Tennessee Walking Horse

Developed in the 18th century, the Tennessee Walking horse was desirable thanks to its ability to cover much ground at a comfortable pace. These horses were used on plantations to carry a rider over long distances whilst pulling a cart with passengers in it. The Tennessee Walking horse performs three basic gaits as well as the famous four- beat running walk. The horse has a straight head and more oversized ears than other horses, plus prominent withers and an agile neck.

The Tennessee Walking horses usually stand from 15 – 16 hands and are solid in color and pinto. As well as trail riding, the Tennessee Walking horse excels at saddle seat classes, Western and English classes.

6.   Thoroughbred

The Thoroughbred is not only classed as the fastest horse but also the most elegant. This breed has huge determination coupled with tremendous energy. Developed in the 1700s in Europe specifically for racing, and this is where their breeding also started with three famous foundation sires, Byerly Turk, Darley Arabian, and Godolphin Arabian.

Thoroughbreds stand between 14.2 – 18 hands and are mostly solid in color, although it is rare to find a roan thoroughbred. This breed is an allrounder and is suitable for many activities, including show jumping, racing, eventing, hunting, polo, dressage, and cross- country.

The Baroque breeds are gaining in popularity, which are centuries old and was bred as war horses. Baroque references the era's style, and examples of these are Lipizzaner, Lusitano, and Andalusian. These are compact horses that can sit dramatically through their hindquarters and are very light on their front ends and therefore, these horses are used to perform dressage.

Popular Pony Breeds

All horses that stand under 14.2 hands high are regarded as ponies. Ponies are distinctive, and there are many popular pony breeds, some of which can be ridden by adults and children. As ponies are a hugely popular choice as first horses for children, it is essential to cover the most popular breeds.

1. Shetland

Standing at the top of all pony breeds is the Shetland, and this is often the breed that springs to mind when you hear the word pony. This breed is one of the smallest and is ideal for children, provided they are well trained. Shetlands have a cheeky personality and have a reputation for being stubborn!

Most Shetlands are 11 hands in height and can be found in many solid colors and pintos. The Shetland is used for driving, as well as Western and English events.

2. Welsh

There are four variations of Welsh ponies, the Welsh Cob, Welsh Mountain Pony, Welsh Pony of Cob Type, and Welsh Pony. Welsh breeds are solid and hardy, which could be why they are popular with farmers. They are also excellent as therapy ponies. Each category varies in height, and as they stand from 12 – 16 hands, some are suitable for adults.

Welsh ponies tend to be chestnut, black, bay, or grey and are the type that can engage in various events such as trail riding, trekking, driving, hunting, and a second pony for a child.

3. Connemara

The Connemara has some Arabian and Thoroughbred traits making them a refined pony. This is Ireland's only indigenous pony with the ancestors believed to have been like the Celtic Pony, Norwegian Ford, and Shetland. There is also some Spanish influence in this breed.

The Connemara tends to stand 13 – 14.2 hands in height, and they are excellent jumpers. Connemara is usually dun, brown, bay, black, or grey, and as well as jumping, they compete in English classes, eventing, driving, cross country, and dressage.

4.   Pony of the Americas

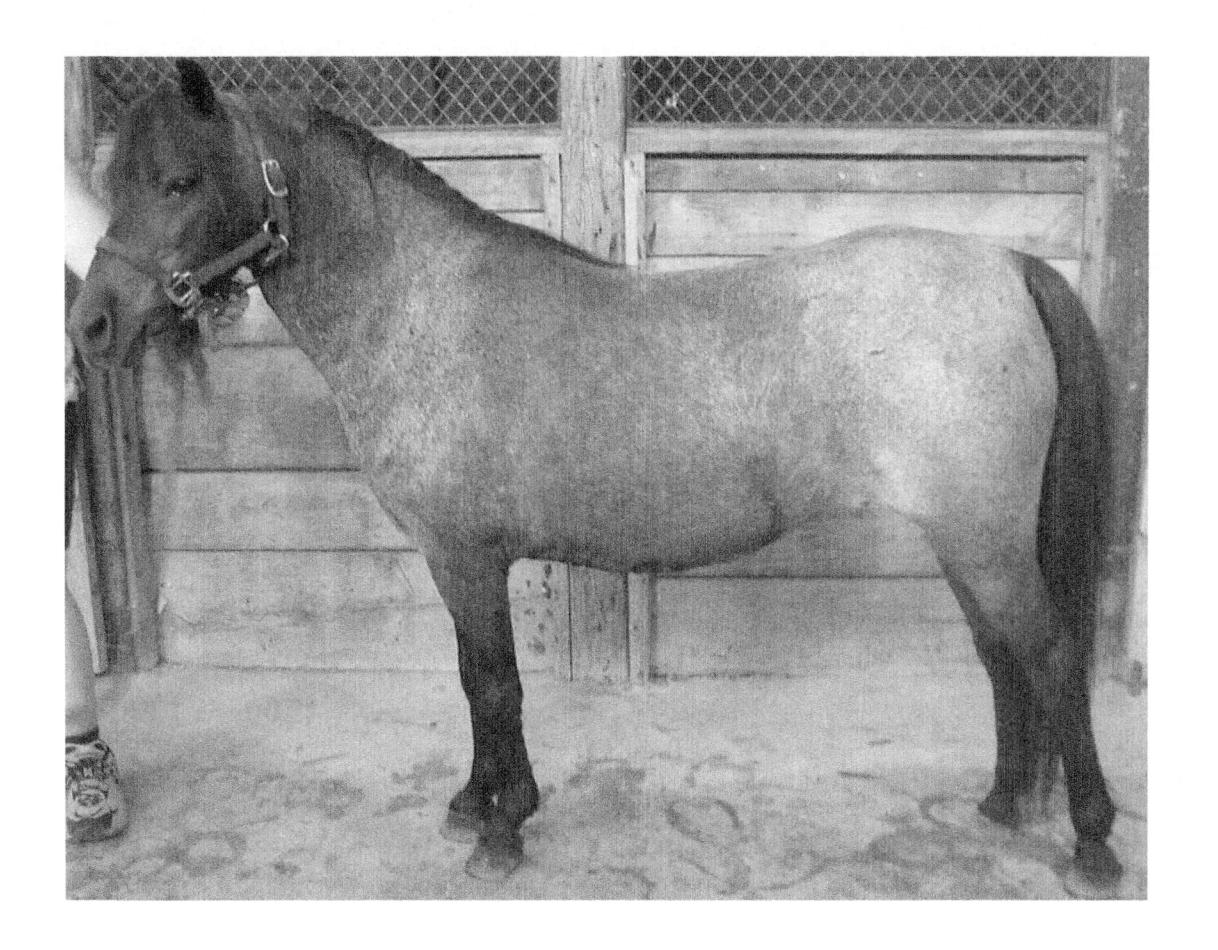

POA (Pony of the Americas) is a cross between Appaloosa and Shetland and often will have typical Appaloosa markings. This pony is popular with children and is excellent for the youth horse show program of the American POA Association. Standing from 11.2 – 14 hands, they are often seen competing in Western and English classes.

Warmbloods

The interest in European Warmbloods has risen due to their versatility and their being ideal for cross country, and dressage. Most Warmblood horses possess the same characteristics, and you could come across as "Cold-blooded", "Warm-blooded" and "Hot-blooded" horses as this is the terminology used to explain their temperament. Cold Blooded horses are usually heavily set and docile draught breeds with the Akhal-Teke, Thoroughbreds, and Andalusians considered to be Hot Blooded.

Most Warmbloods are the result of crossing a light riding

horse or Thoroughbred with draught breeds. If you are interested in a Warmblood, there are a number for you to choose from including, Dutch Warmbloods, Irish Sporthorses, Swedish Warmbloods, Holsteiners, and Russian Warmbloods as well as the ones that will be described more fully below. Warmbloods excel in numerous equestrian events such as driving, dressage, cross-country, jumping, and as hunters.

1. Hanoverian

The Hanoverian is a popular Warmblood breed and one of the most popular riding horses. Inspired by King George 11 in 1735 when he instructed the Celle stud in Lower Saxony to produce a coach horse that would also be good for agricultural work. This horse went on to become a military mount. Modern Hanoverian horses are powerful and have big, springy movements and they are calm and level-headed.

Hanoverians range in height from 15.3 – 17.2 hands and although they were predominately chestnut, there are other colors. This breed excels in dressage, showjumping, cross-country, and eventing making it a sort after equestrian breed.

2. Trakehner

In 1732 Friedrich Wilhelm 1 of Prussia got all his horses together at his Trakehn stud with the idea of producing a light cavalry horse. By 1940 there were about 80,000 Trakehners, many of which went on to win steeplechases and become gold medallists. Prussia was invaded in 1945, and many of the horses died however, due to several evacuation attempts approximately 1,000 reached safety in West Germany. The breed underwent vigorous evaluations so they could be entered into the studbook and are now a balanced, free-moving, and elegant breed.

Trakehner's stand between 15.3 – 17 hands is usually either black, bay, chestnut, or grey in color. Due to their spirit, they are not a horse that is recommended for a beginner, and they excel in the fields of endurance and dressage.

Colors and Markings

The best way to understand the colors of horses is to see them, but it is important that you remember that each color can vary in shade quite a lot dependent on the horse. To try and make these easier the following color descriptions will be followed by a picture of that colored horse.

1. **Cremellos or White**

White horses are Cremellos or Albinos. There is a saying, that all white horses are grey, and it is true that some white horses are grey, but it is worth knowing that there are also Cremellos and Albinos. These horses have pink muzzles and light hooves with brown or blue eyes.

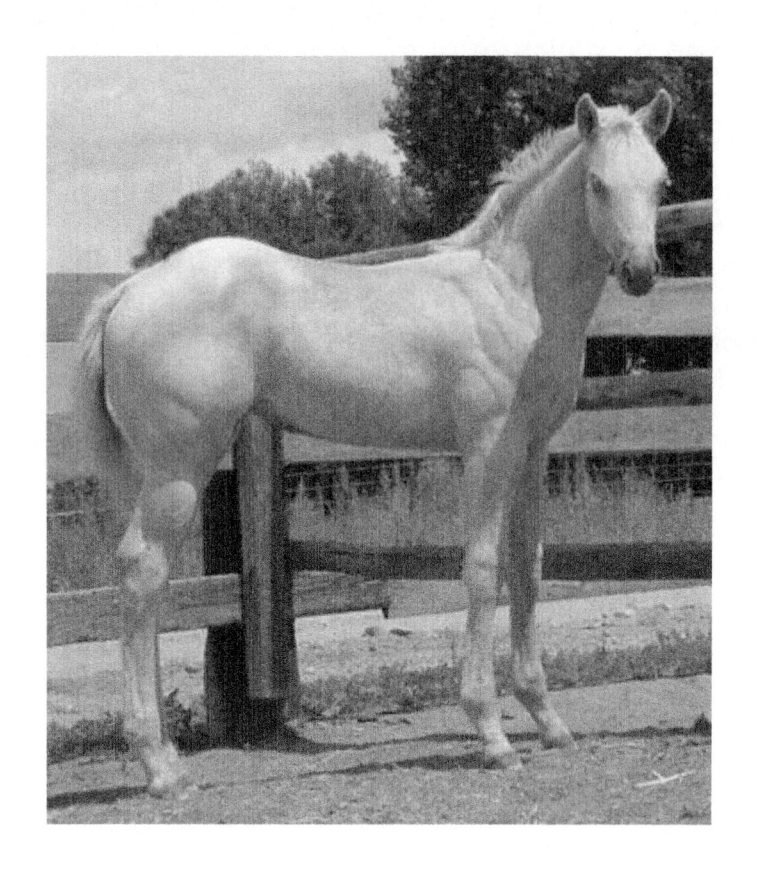

2. **Grey**

There are various shades of grey as some horses can be almost white whereas others can be dark and dappled. The dark and white hairs of the horse mix and produce a grey appearance. Foals are often born in a solid color such as charcoal or brown and they then lighten as they grow older. Unlike white horse's grey horses have black skin. Grey is not a natural color as it has been born from genetics and grey horses carry a certain gene which masks their true color. The Lipizzaner breeds are traditionally grey but there are rare instances where they have been born black or bay.

3. Pinto

Pinto markings are usually patches of dark against white and like the markings found on the Paint horses. There are only certain horse breeds that display pinto markings.

4. **Palomino**

Palominos have a gold, yellow body color with flaxen white mane and tails.

5. **Dun**

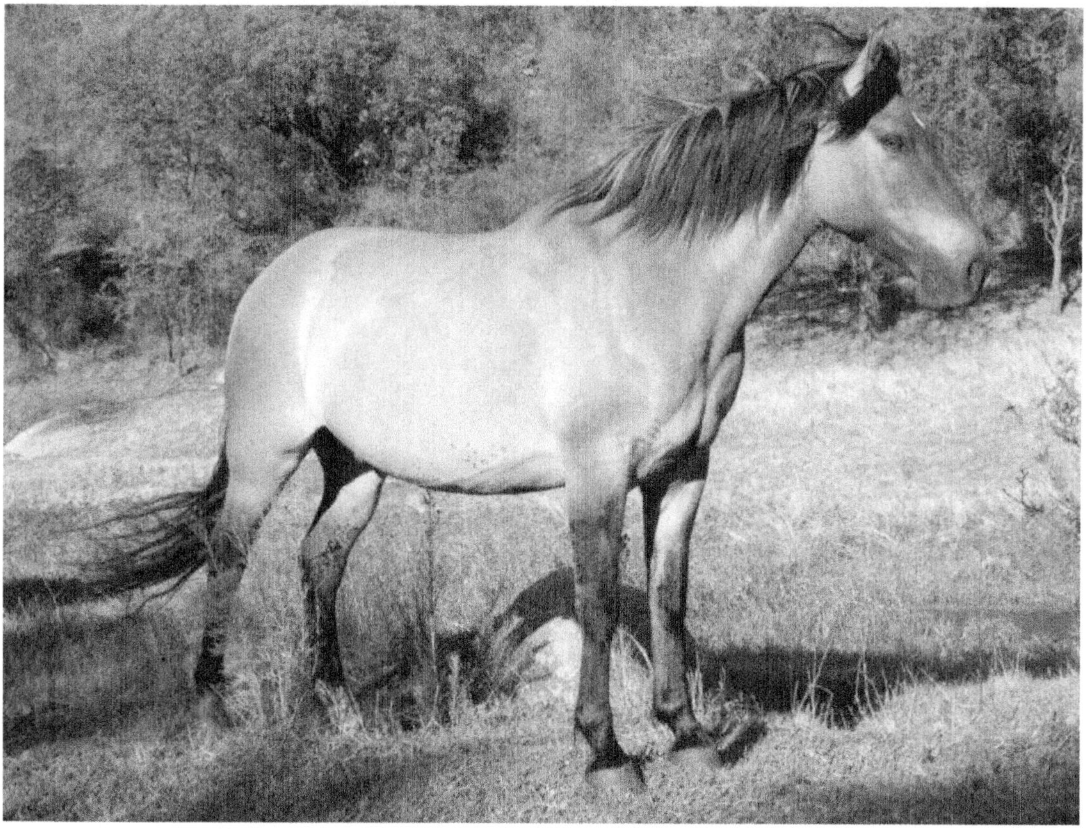

Dun is thought of as one of the nearest colors to that of "wild" horses. This could be because of the dorsal stripe and striping which appears on the lower legs of Dun-colored horses.

6. Chestnut

Chestnut horses have a distinctive red color on their bodies and their manes and tails. There are huge variations of chestnut starting with very light to a dark almost liver color.

7. Bay

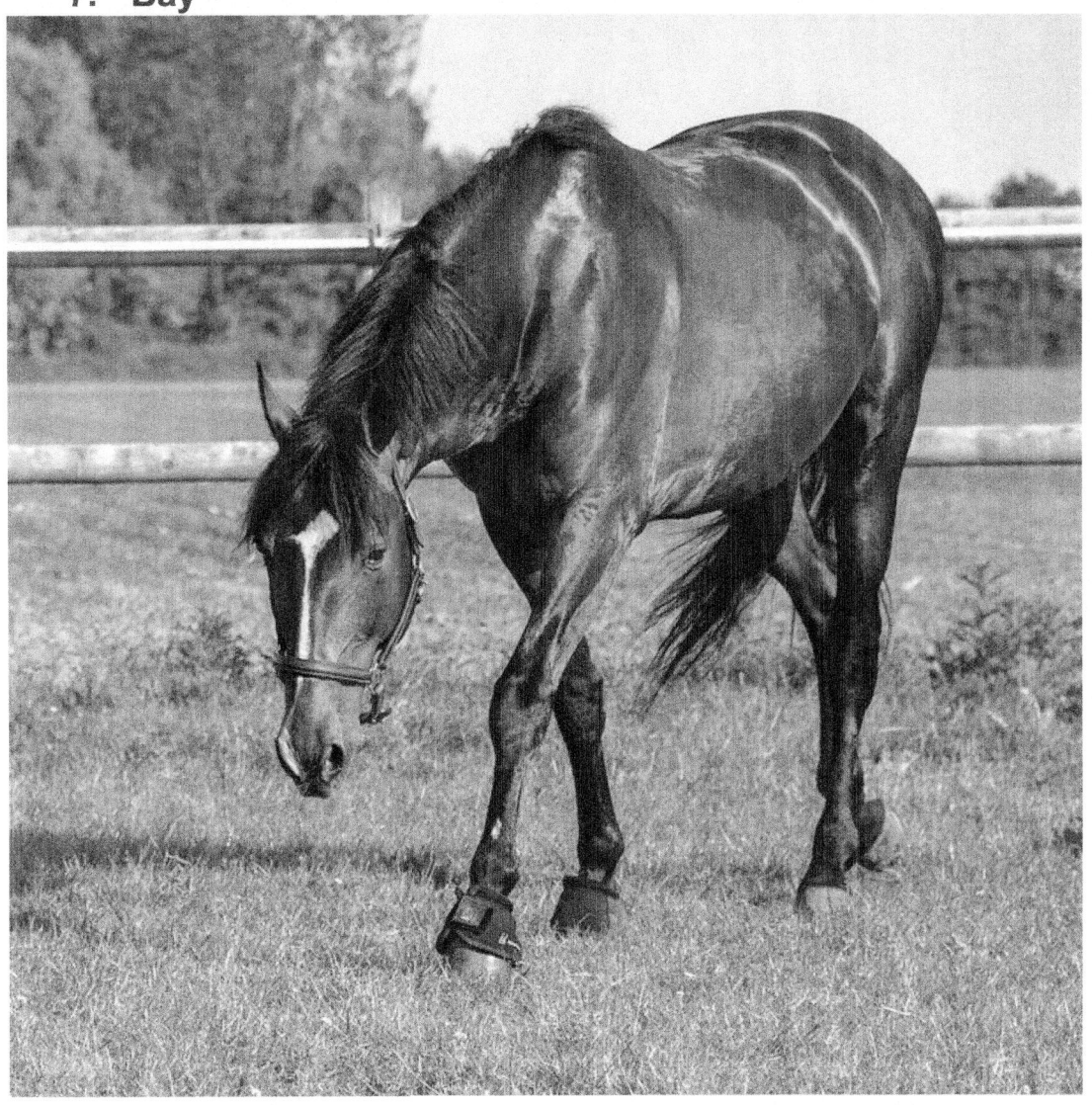

Bay horses have a brown/red-brown body, but their manes and tails are always black. They also always have black on the lower parts of their legs; the amount of black does vary from one bay horse to another.

8. **Brown**

Brown horses have brown bodies and legs, they should also have a brown muzzle, flank, and upper legs. They may have some black on their lower legs and their manes and tails are also black.

9. Roan

There are a variety of shades of roan including strawberry roan, red and blue roans. Roan horses have a uniform mix of white and red hairs or white and black hairs. Roan horses often also have a black or brown head with black legs and their mane and tails can be either chestnut or black.

10. Black

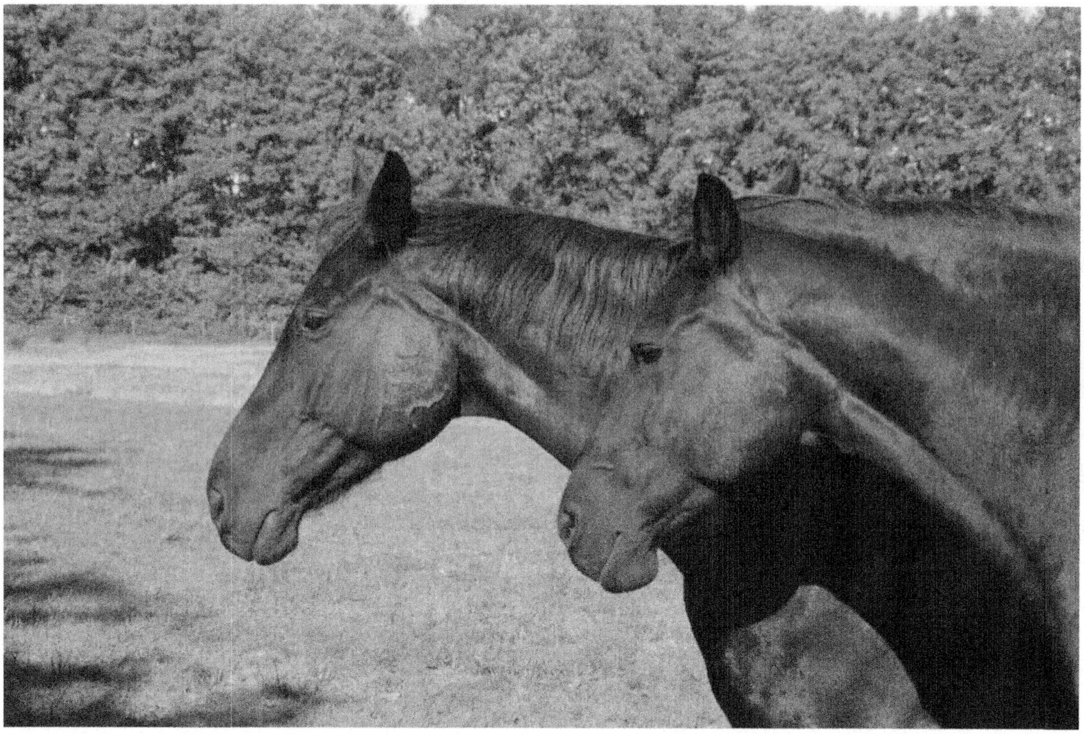

A truly black horse is one that is solid black with no white on the body elsewhere, black horses also have pure black manes and tails.

Markings

Most horses have distinguishable markings, and it is their markings that can be thought of as the fingerprint of the horse, as there are no two horses that share identical markings.

Each marking has a name which is used amongst equine professionals from vets to trainers. Each marking can have subtle variations as every horse is genetically different.

Face Markings

1. **Blaze**

A blaze is a white area that runs down along the bridge of a horse's nose and is often in the form of a white stripe.

2. **Snip**

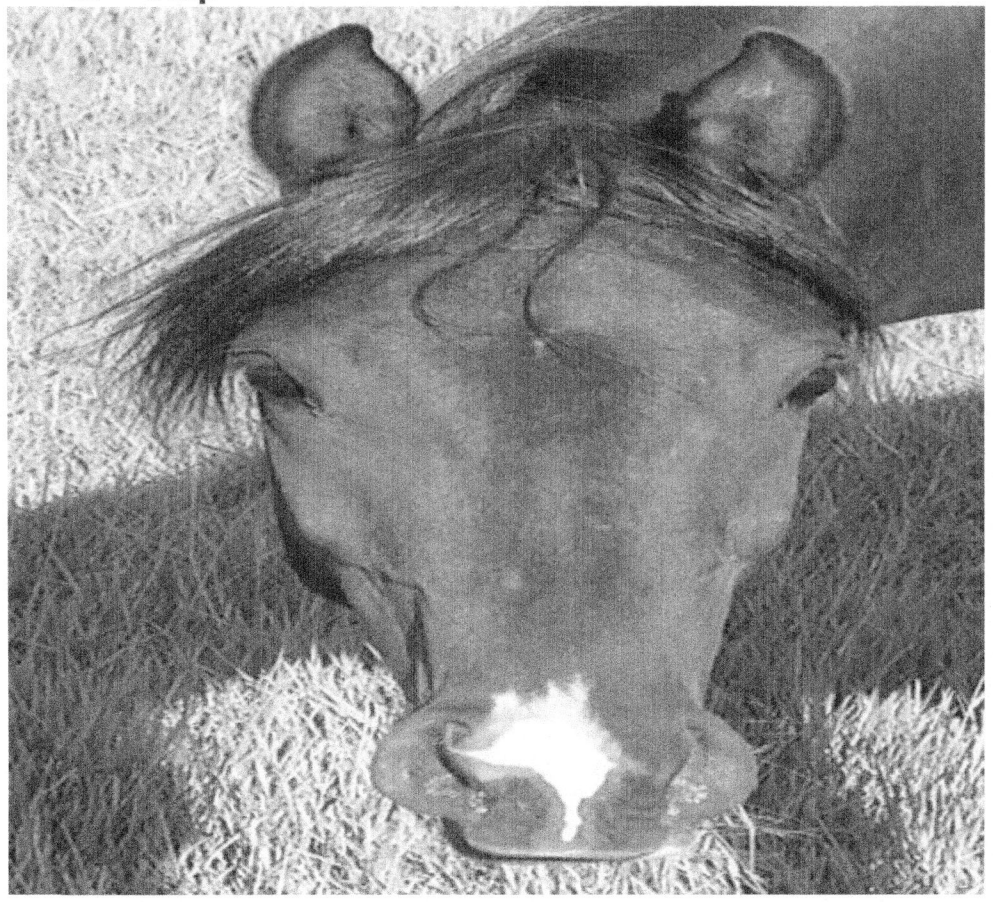

3. **Star**

A snip refers to a small white spot that can be found on the horse's muzzle above its lip.

A star is exactly that, a white spot which can be star shaped and found on the horse's forehead.

4. Stripe

snip.

Leg Markings

A stripe refers to a narrow white stripe which runs down the center of the horse's face, the stripe is far thinner than a blaze even though they are both located in the same area of the face.

Many horses have a combination of muddled facial markings such as a star with a stripe and

In the same way, as facial markings horse also has different leg markings such as:

1. **Coronet**

On a horse, this is a small white band that is just above the top of the hoof, where the coronet is located.

2. **Half Cannon**

A half cannon is white on the leg that extends halfway up the middle of the cannon bone. The half cannon is shorter than a stocking and longer than a sock.

3. **Half Pastern**

A half pastern is where the white extends halfway up the pastern (obvious I know).

4. **Sock**

A sock is when the white extends two-thirds of the way up the cannon of the leg.

5. Stocking

A stocking is where there is white that extends from the hoof up to the knee or the hock.

Chapter 3 – Getting Ready for Your Ride

Many people think when it comes to horseback riding, it is the horse that does all the work, and whilst they will do most of the work, they do not do all of it. When you ride, you have plenty to do both mentally and physically; for this reason, you should prepare yourself both physically and mentally to do this sport justice.

Riding is about finesse and skill, but you also need endurance, strong muscles, flexibility, and balance. When you start learning to ride, you begin at a walk, which does require a degree of flexibility. When you move on to trotting, cantering, or galloping, you need flexibility, stamina, and strength. You need strength to hold yourself in the correct position when trotting, cantering, and galloping and the power when you are trotting to rise up and down in the stirrups if you are riding in English.

Riding will be more enjoyable if you are in good physical shape, and it is easier on the horse. Fit riders can hold themselves in position and balance, whereas an unfit rider is a burden for a horse to carry as they feel like a dead weight on their back.

Before you start to ride, it is a good idea to prepare your body. You need to ensure that you are the right weight and should begin developing your muscle strength, stamina and increasing your flexibility. You should put yourself on a health regime a few weeks before you start riding, and although your instructor will be easy when you start, this will not last for too long; take it from one who knows! Riding will help your fitness, but you want to be sure that you will not end up so sore after a lesson that you cannot walk for the next day or two.

Losing a pound or two

Weight is a complex subject, and most of us have struggled with our weight at some point in our lives; and although you may not want to think about your weight, it is important when horseback riding. The first thing you may find if you are overweight is that you cannot get comfortable or feel secure in the saddle. By losing weight not only will horseback riding be far more enjoyable, but it will be easier on your horse too. Fit riders can hold their position and balance easily. Unfit riders are a burden for the horse to carry as they feel like a dead weight.

Getting on and off

Getting up into a saddle takes a lot of upper body strength, and the more you weigh, the harder this will be. Many riders cannot mount without standing on a mounting block or something tall, this is fine, and is my preferred technique as it puts less strain on the horse's back (I am not that heavy – just for the record!). It would be best to get on a horse unassisted as you could find yourself somewhere with no suitable object to use as your mounting block.

Energy

Riding requires endurance and a certain amount of strength, and if you are or have ever been overweight, you will know how hard it is to take part in any strenuous activity without getting out of breath. A healthy weight is essential for horseback riding as you will find it much easier to keep up with your horse.

Aerobic exercise and endurance

You need good stamina for horseback riding, and if you are planning to ride English or take up trail riding, endurance is vital to you. English style riders spend a lot of their time going up and down in the saddle (also known as posting), which requires a lot of stamina. Trail riders spend hours in the saddle and therefore need the endurance to stay in the saddle for long periods.

Strength

The muscles that you will use the most in horseback riding are your arms, legs, and stomach. The stronger you are in these areas, the easier it will be for you to communicate your movements to the horse and keep your balance in the saddle.

Arms

Strong arms will make it a lot easier for you to pull yourself into the saddle and strong arms are a necessity if you are riding English style as you need to keep constant contact with the horse's mouth through your reins. Whilst you never pull on a horse's mouth, strength is required so you can keep your arms in the correct position for lengthy periods.

Legs

One of the essential attributes for any rider is leg strength because when you are on a horse, you use the pressure from your legs to command instructions and keep your balance in the saddle. The more you ride, the stronger your legs will be.

Abdomen

Your abdomen or stomach muscles are the center of your balance when you are in the saddle. Having strong muscles will help you maintain the correct posture and keep you stable when your horse moves.

Another great way to get in shape for riding is to enroll in a Pilates or Yoga class as both these disciplines will teach you a low-impact body workout that stretches and strengthens the muscles you need for riding.

Flexibility

When you ride, flexibility is vital because if your muscles stretch easily, you can move freely with your horse, plus you are far more unlikely to injure yourself during a vigorous training session. You should find that you are not sore afterward.

It's all in mind

Horseback riding is as much of a mental activity as it is a physical one. Your brain must coordinate your body so you can balance and send signals to the horse. Having a positive mental attitude will give your horse confidence and make them realize that you are in charge.

Being the leader

Have you ever thought how fabulous it is that a horse lets you ride it? Nothing is stopping them from throwing you off and running away, but they don't. Horses view people as leaders, but they will soon determine whether you have what it takes to be in charge.

When dealing with horses, you need to be confident and consistent whether you are riding or leading. You should be firm but gentle and make sure the horse listens to you and ensure they do not get away with anything. If you ask the horse to stand still, then make sure that it does and do not let it walk off until you are ready. If you let a horse do what they want, you will set yourself up, and you will then do what the horse wants to do, and there is a great chance this will not be what you want it to be!

Fear

If you rode as a child like me, the chances are that you will remember having no fear regardless of how big the horse was because you trusted it with your well-being. As you get older, anxiety can get into your mind. I have fabulous childhood memories where I cantered through woods without a care in the world. Now when I repeat this experience,

I find myself thinking that something terrible could happen. Many adults want to ride, but the fear of getting hurt stops them. This change could be because as adults, we have others dependent on our staying in one piece. It is natural if you are starting horseback riding or have already started, and you are feeling a little scared. You should not ignore this feeling, but you do need to think that fear can hold you back and stop you from enjoying what you want to do, and in some cases, you can also transfer your anxiety to your horse.

Time for Lessons

To enjoy horseback riding, you need to do it properly, and this is the best advice I can give you. I imagine you need to know more about horseback riding before you begin, but not everybody has this mindset. Some people get on a horse for the first time and expect they will know what to do; after all, they have seen others riding, and it doesn't look that hard! The idea of taking lessons does not cross their mind, but would they go downhill skiing without instruction? I don't think so! But these people will climb on a horse without any idea of how to control it.

Some people may believe that as horses are animals with brains, they should not need any training as they figure that the horse will know what to do. However, the fact that a horse has a brain is why you need lessons to start. Convincing a horse to do what you want to do and not letting them do what they want to do takes skill.

Finding the most suitable stable

You have decided that you are going to start riding and as so the first step is to find a good place to have lessons. There are various ways to search for a suitable stable where you can learn horseback riding, such as:

Word of mouth: The best way to find anything comes from recommendations from other people that have been in the place you are right now. Talk to the people that ride at the stables, talk to local tack shop owners or customers and the chances are you will find a suitable stable with great instructors. Although we live in a world surrounded by the internet, I suggest visiting the stables before you commit, regardless of how you find them.

What you need for horseback riding

You are now at the point where you have found the stables that you feel happy with. It would help if you got yourself ready to begin lessons, and whilst you do not need to go overboard and buy everything horsey, there are some essentials that you should never forget as they can make the difference between life and death.

If you are a beginner, there is no need to rush out and buy everything, as you will find that you will not need that much to get you started. You probably have some bare minimums in your wardrobes, such as long non-slick pants and heeled shoes with a closed toe. As a beginner, you are likely to be riding a bombproof horse or pony. You must remember that horses have a mind of their own and are big animals; therefore, I would suggest investing or at least borrowing some minimal safety equipment because you can find yourself on the floor in a matter of seconds.

You must have a helmet, and you need a helmet that is designed specifically for horseback riding. You may think you can use a bicycle helmet, but this will not protect you adequately if you fall off and brain injuries are life-threatening. You may also want to invest in a safety vest as this will protect your vital organs, and you will fall off one day, particularly as you gain experience and try more advanced things. Wearing a vest will take some shock if you hit the floor and will certainly make the difference between being winded or cracking a rib or two!

Grooming

Grooming not only makes your horse look good but will give you pride when you ride but grooming also helps you build a bond with your horse and keep them healthy. Grooming lets you give your horse a full going over and spot things that should not be there. It is a real bonus if you enjoy grooming because horses are dirty critters that love to roll and need grooming daily. Cleaning a half-ton of horse who has been milling around in dirt and dust may not be your idea of fun, but grooming can be one of the most rewarding parts of horseback riding.

Before you can begin grooming, you need to assemble a grooming kit and make sure everything is clean and in working order. A minimum grooming kit should contain a stiff brush, a soft brush, a mane and tail brush, a sponge, cloth, a small towel, a sweat scraper, a rubber curry comb, a shedding blade, and a hoof pick.

Horses are dirty, and it clings to their coats, and you will find that you need to use elbow grease to get the horse's coat shiny and clean. You will develop your grooming regime; however, I always find that by undertaking the following, nothing gets left out!

1. Clean out the horses' hooves with the hoof pick to remove anything that has

   become embedded in their feet.

2. Use the curry comb to bring the dirt to the surface of the horses' coat by using

   a circular motion.

3. Use the stiff brush to brush the dirt into the air using short strokes in the direction the coat goes.

4. Use the soft brush to remove any remaining dust and use short strokes in the direction the fur lays.

5. Wipe the horse's body down with the cloth.

6. Use the cloth to clean inside the nostrils where you will find dirt tends to accumulate.

7. Use the soft brush again to gently groom the horse's head using long, gentle

 strokes.

8. Use the mane and tail brush to run through and make sure they are tangle- free.

After following this process, not only will your horse feel fabulous, but it will look good too.

Leg Wrapping and its purpose

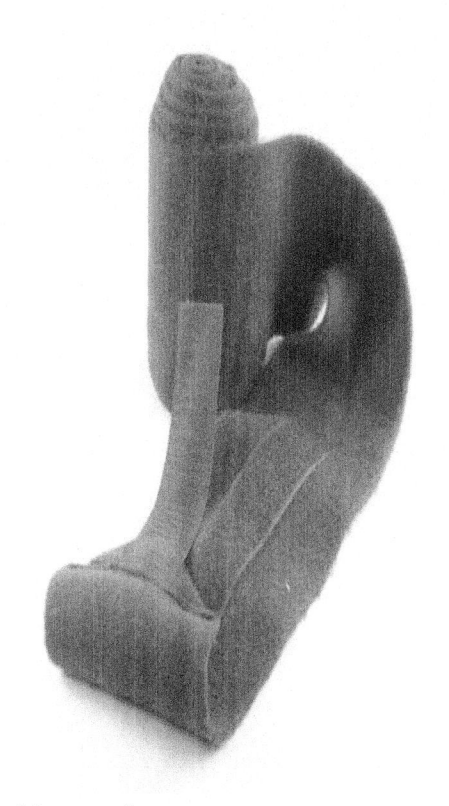

Horse leg wraps, support the ligaments and tendons while protecting the horse from abrasions, covering wounds, and keeping flies off the horses' legs. There are various reasons for a horse to be wrapped, which may not be obvious to onlookers.

Uses of horse leg wraps There are different styles and uses for leg wraps; some are used during a workout or when the horse travels, whereas others are designed for the horse to wear if they are injured or kept in a stable or small field/paddock.

Before you use wraps, you need to seek help from an experienced horse rider or instructor who can teach you the right way to wrap your horses' leg, as getting this wrong can seriously hurt your horse.

Rear leg wraps

Wraps on a horse's hind legs are used mainly by racehorse trainers and are known as rundown bandages, preventing interference injuries and preventing abrasions caused by friction.

Front leg wraps

Racehorses also use front leg wraps to protect against interference injuries and give additional tendon support. Interference injuries come when one of the horse's limbs meet another limb whilst they are running.

There are many reasons why a horse's legs can hit one another, and this ranges from conformation, improper shoes, issues with fitness, or the way the horse strides. Even the healthiest horse can misstep, causing their legs to catch against each other and cause an injury.

Interference injuries

An interference injury can range from rubbed hair to a deep cut and cause the horse pain, bruising, and swelling, particularly around their fetlock joints.

Brushing

Brushing is an interference injury that occurs when the opposite limbs of the horse come into contact. For example, a connection can arise from the knee to the hoof in the front limbs, whereas the strike is usually to the fetlock in the rear legs.

Overreaching

When a horse overreaches, it is striking the lower part of the front leg with the toe of its rear leg and can see the horse out of action for a considerable amount of time.

Leg wraps provide tendon support

No research or proof has shown that wraps provide extra support to a horse's tendons; some trainers believe they do; however, they provide support if the horse has a tendon injury.

Leg wraps increase the temperature of the horse's legs which can be both positive and negative. There will be times that a vet may suggest heat will help tendon injuries; however, overall, heat will cause more harm than good.

Should horses wear leg wraps when being transported?

It is advisable to wrap your horse's legs when loaded in a vehicle because horses need to move; otherwise, their legs will swell, but the pressure applied from the wraps increases the blood flow and counteracts any swelling. By wrapping the legs, you protect the horse from acute injuries when the lorry is moving.

Types of leg wraps

There are two main types of leg wraps that you can use on horses, and they both have a specific use.

Polo wraps are worn for support when competing in a competition or exercising.

Stable/Standing wraps are used to treat swelling and supporting tendons, apply pressure, and treat wounds. Stable/Standing wraps consist of two layers, the inner is thickly quilted, which distributes pressure, and the outer layer holds the inner layer firmly in place.

Longeing/Lungeing

If a horse stays in its stable due to bad weather, it is essential to warm them up before you ride them. Typically, these are horses with a lot of energy that they need to get rid of before being ridden. Longeing or lungeing is the ideal way to determine whether your horse is safe to ride.

Once horses get moving, they may let out a buck or two, and by allowing them this time to get rid of their excitement, they will settle, and you can then put them through their paces. Working on the basic gaits in each direction will warm up the horse's muscles whilst calming them down.

Longeing and lungeing are the same thing, and when you are longeing your horse, you are aiming to get the horse to follow the long line (longeing rope) and allow you to drive them forwards by standing behind their shoulder. It would be best if you also made sure that the horse's head is looking a little towards you with their eyes focused on you so that they listen and partake fully.

When longeing, you should direct the horse with your right hand if the horse is going right and the left hand if they are going round in a left circle. Many horses will want to go either one way or the other, and this shows that they have not been worked so much in the weaker direction, but you must work the horse equally in both directions.

Teaching a horse to longe can take time and patience, but once they understand, this is a technique you can use in many situations. However, there will come a time when the horse starts to work around you, and you will only need to vocalize the commands. On average, 20 minutes of longeing should be enough to warm your horse up before you ride. Anymore and you could end up damaging the horse as longeing is hard on their joints.

Bridles and Saddles

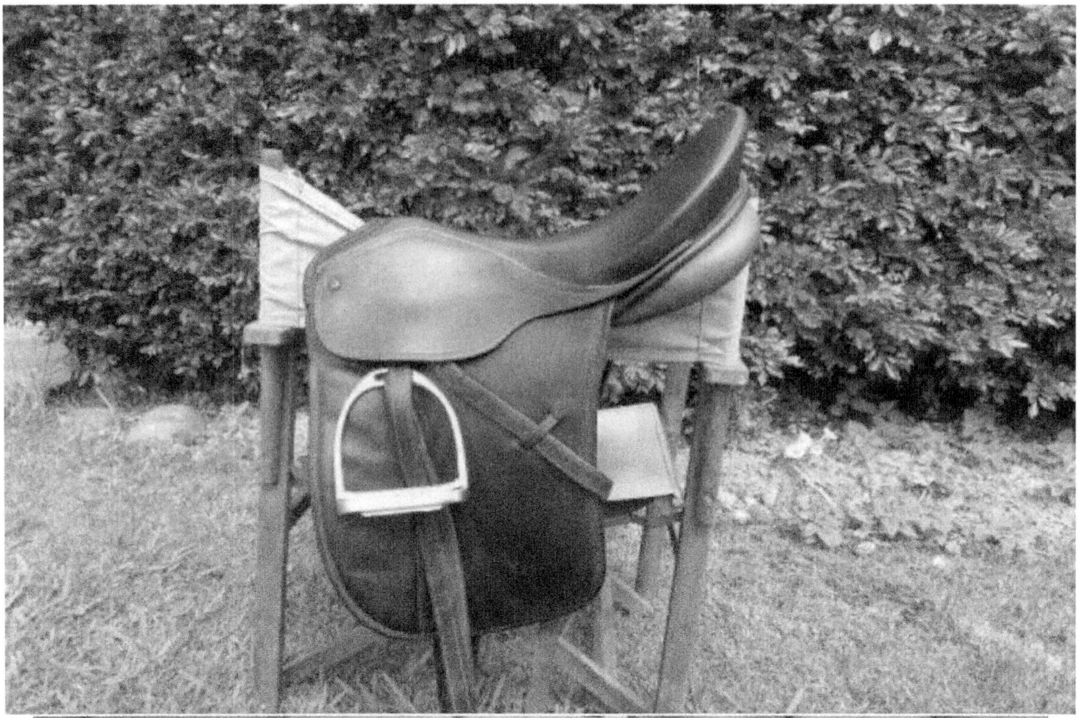

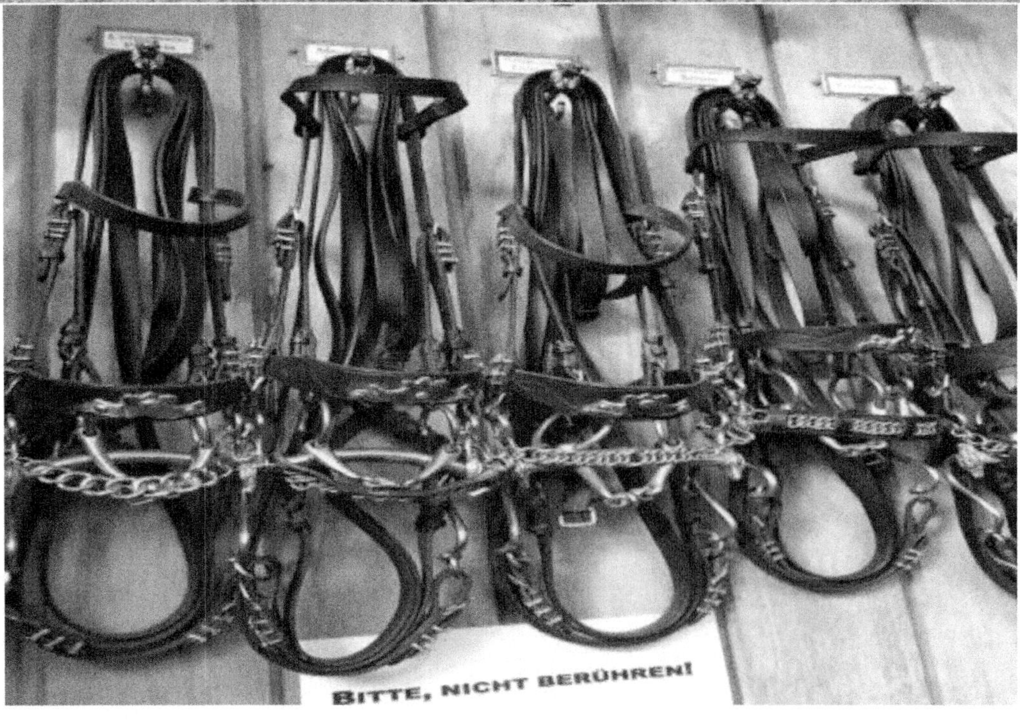
BITTE, NICHT BERÜHREN!

When it comes to tacking up your horse, you should put the saddle on first only because your horse needs to be tied up, and you cannot tie the horse up with the reins of the bridle as they could pull back, hurting their mouth and the tack.

When you are ready to put on the horse's bridle, you should remove the halter and fasten this around the neck. If you are using an English bridle, be sure to check that the throat latch and noseband are undone, and if you are using a Western bridle, the throatlatch should be undone if there is one.

How to put on a bridle

Although it may seem challenging to begin with, it is easy to bridle a horse if you follow the steps below:

1. Put the reins over the horse's head and let them lie on the neck.

2. Stand on the horse's left, with the bit in your left hand and the top of the

    bridle in your right.

3. Place your right hand on the forelock holding the bridle between the ears.

4. Open the horse's mouth and gently put in the bit; if the horse doesn't want to open their mouth, you can gently put your thumb in its mouth, which should get them to open.

5. Once the bit is in the horse's mouth, slide the ears into the top of the bridle

    and pull out their forelock so it is on the top of the browband.

6. Do up the buckles on the throat latch and noseband, and you should be able to put two fingers between the horse and the fixed throatlatch.

7. Remove the halter, and you are ready to go!

How to put on a saddle

When it comes to the saddle, it must fit properly into the horse's back. By following the

tips below, you should find you get it right all the time.

1. Place the saddle pad on the horse's back to the front of the withers, then slide

    it back into the correct position.

2. Put the saddle over the saddle pad and pull it up so that it is not tight against the withers. If you are using a Western saddle, you need to flip the right stirrup and girth over the top of the saddle, whereas on an English saddle, you will slide the stirrups to the top of the leathers. With an English saddle, you will want approximately three inches of pad visible at both the front and

rear of the saddle; for the Western saddle, you will have about three inches to the front but maybe more at the back. You can tell if the saddle is in the correct place as the girth will fit behind the horse's elbow.

3. The girth on a Western saddle attaches on the right side, but this can vary on an English saddle. If you are riding using the English saddle, you will secure the girth to the right side and attach it on the left side; however, on a Western saddle, you take the girth and stirrup from the top of the saddle and reach under to the left side to attach the girth.

4. When you secure the girth on an English saddle, you gradually move the holes up slowly. On a Western saddle, you loop the latigo strap through the D-ring on the girth, continue looping until you have approximately one foot of latigo left and the needle on the D-ring fits into the hole; the excess gets stored in the latigo keeper.

5. Next, you check your stirrup lengths, placing your hand under the flap above the stirrup leather, then using your left hand, place the stirrup against your extended arm; the stirrup should reach your armpit. Once you get on the horse, you can determine whether the stirrups are comfortable. On an English saddle, the stirrups should sit by your ankle, whereas in a Western saddle, you need to be able to stand and balance for a few seconds.

Chapter 4 – Safe Riding

When you are riding, you want to ensure that you are as safe as possible. Horses are large animals and humans cannot match them when it comes to strength.

There are various precautions and measures that you can take to make sure that riding is not only fun, but you are staying safe too.

Horses are unpredictable animals, and there are some typical behaviors that I hope you will never encounter; however, you must be prepared should they unexpectedly occur. These are things such as rearing, bucking, spooking, and running away, and these things can happen to the most proficient horsemen and women, even those that have been riding for years. The key to keeping safe in these situations is knowing what to expect and how you can deal with it.

Safety Clothing

You need to dress appropriately for horseback riding. As you get more experienced, you will understand how important safety is when riding and cringe at those who believe that trainers and shorts are the correct attire. Regardless of how hot it may be, this is a big no, no.

Western Riders

Western riders are considered appropriately dressed when they have jeans, cowboy boots, and a shirt that is not lose or baggy, and even t-shirts are fine as long as they are tucked in and not flowing. When you are riding western style, it would be so easy for a baggy shirt to get caught on trees, the saddle horn, fencing, and everything else you happen to snag it on. Most western riders do not wear a riding hat, but they are safe, and if you choose to wear one, it will be acceptable. Many riding hat manufacturers make riding hats appealing and more western in style, complete with conchos and leather. Some riding hats appear to be cowboy hats complete with a chin strap. You should always wear a riding hat regardless of the style you are riding in, riders are thrown from western saddles as quickly as they can English ones, and I have been grateful for a riding hat on many occasions. It is also vital to ensure that your riding hat is certified and fit for purpose, do not be fooled into thinking that a bicycle helmet can replace it as this does not undergo the rigorous training and testing that riding hats do.

English Riders

Riding English style, you are likely to be the most comfortable in jodhpurs, along with a pair of field or long boots. Beige breeches and tall boots are more formal attire used when showing the horse and these are teamed with a white shirt, tie, and show jacket. Dressage riders wear white jodhpurs, tie, any shirt as it will not be seen, and a specific dressage coat.

When you are riding casually, you can either wear jodhpurs or jeans with paddock boots. It is worth noting that you can buy jeans that are for horseback riding. Many riders opt for jodhpurs and tall boots when they are casually riding as they are so comfortable. If riders prefer to wear jeans, they could wear schooling chaps or half-chaps over them, and once again, they must ensure that everything is tucked in.

All clothing will be weather dependent, so if it is cold, you will want to add ample layers with gloves and a coat. It might be an idea to also consider wearing extra thick socks. Otherwise, a t-shirt and close-fitting garments that will keep you cool are a must if it is warm. Just remember to always put your safety first.

Riding Hat

When horseback riding, you should always use a certified riding hat, and you should be mindful that many English riding hats are for dress and showing only, and many of these are not certified. Riding hats come in different styles. Certification means that the riding hat has undergone testing to improve impact absorption and increased strength to withstand a bang to the head. Your riding hat should fit properly and be complete with a harness or chin strap. If you are thrown from a horse with a riding hat on, the chances are that it may not be as strong as it should be, and many riding hat manufacturers will replace your riding hat for free if this has happened. The other point worth mentioning is that you need to purchase a riding hat that is purely for equestrians.

Body Protectors

If you are going to be jumping, there are particular body protector vests that you may want to consider buying. Body protectors are a necessity (in my opinion) for any child. The vests are padded and provide a certain degree of protection to the rib cage, collar bones, and spine.

Jewelry

Obviously, you are not going to get all dressed up in your party clothes to go down to the stables, however, there are some that do! Removing your silver and gold may sound stupid, but I need to tell you anyway: Do not wear your jewelry around horses.

Jewelry in particular large rings, dangly earrings, and bangles can get caught on any part of the bridle or saddle. You can also catch your jewelry on a variety of objects in the stables such as gate latches, saddle racks, and so on.

Clothes not to wear when riding

Every day a rider is hurt when horseback riding because they wear the wrong attire. The following are the clothing and footwear that you should never wear horseback riding:

- Sandals

- Open-toed shoes

- Shoes with no heel

- Slip-on shoes

- Shorts

- Baggy Shirts

- Baggy trousers

I would also advise against wearing any of your best clothes, as you will get dirty.

Now you have an insight into what you should do to ensure your safety, and we will move on to the unpredictable behaviors of horses that you need to be aware of.

Spooking

At some point, when you are horseback riding, the horse will spook; how dramatic this depends on how you react. Horses are intelligent animals, and they are always alert for anything that may come from nowhere, meaning that they will spook easily. Older trusted horses have become desensitized to the scariest and noisy things and are often referred to as being bombproof.

Usually, when a horse spooks, they shy away from something and sidestep or hop slightly to the side. Other horses will spook and bolt away from whatever has scared them.

If the spook is very dramatic, it is easy for the rider to fall off, and if your horse does spook at something, you need to remain calm and balanced. You can usually feel when a horse is about to spook as their whole-body tenses, and when this happens, you should turn the horse to face whatever is scaring them and talk quietly whilst giving them a reassuring pat on the neck. These actions are often enough to calm your horse down, and if you find that your horse refuses to pass the object, I suggest getting off and walking them past.

Some horses will use a spook to their advantage as they know that you will dismount because you did when they spooked before. The dismounting is a reward to a horse that spooks. To ride through a spook and get the horse past the frightening object or situation, you should start by putting both calves on them with a constant squeeze, as applying calf pressure often calms a nervous horse. Ride shoulder-fore, with the horse, bent away from the object whilst maintaining the pressure with your calves.

Therefore, if your horse is refusing to pass a tent that is on your right, bend it slightly to the left by squeezing your left rein and applying your left leg. Use your seat to drive the horse forward, keep pressing with your calves, and move forward using your seat whilst maintaining the shoulder-fore past the scary object.

Bucking

Bucking occurs when a horse has too much energy; alternatively, they may have learned that this is also the quickest way to get rid of their rider! If a horse is in pain, it may also buck, which will usually be down to a kidney problem or an ill-fitted saddle. If you try a different saddle and the problem persists, it is wise to have the vet check that the horse is not suffering from an illness.

If you find your horse bucks a lot when you are riding them, you could try longeing/lunging before you are getting on to ensure that they are properly warmed up and have expended all their energy. Remember, this will not train the horse that they should not buck whilst you are on board, so always keep your wits about you! It is also wise to check the saddle is not pinching.

When horseback riding, if you get bucked off and are not seriously hurt, you need to get straight back on the horse. This shows the horse that bucking will not be tolerated, and it is not a way to end the ride. If you cannot get back on yourself, then get someone to do this for you. It is always best to get back on as this will ensure that you do not harbor any fears about being bucked off.

To get a strong buck, the horse needs to drop its head as this enables the horse to lift its hindquarters high. If you stop the horse from dropping its head down, it will not have the leverage required to give a strong buck. Applying your legs and driving the horse forwards is preferable as this way, the horse will provide a rolling buck rather than a demanding, high buck that makes it difficult for you to stay in the saddle. Keep your back straight and strong, use your legs to drive the horse forwards, and do not let the horse pull the reins from your hands.

More advanced riders can also use discipline to overcome bucking. A swift smack on the bottom when the horse bucks will help them understand that bucking is not acceptable under any circumstances.

Rearing

One of the most dangerous and bad habits a horse can have is to rear. Rearing is when a horse stands on its hind legs and lifts its front feet off the ground. Some horses will rear at things that are in front of them otherwise they can also rear if you are using a harsh and incorrect bit. When a horse has pain in its mouth, the only known way to get away from the pain is to go up in the air.

Rearing when being ridden is a dangerous habit that is never acceptable. If a horse rears when you ask them to do something they do not want to do, you must wait it out and shift all of your weight forward. If you shift your weight back or pull on the reins, you will be at serious risk of the horse falling backward on you.

You may find that you need to seek professional help for a rearing horse. But, if you are on a horse that rears, try to keep them moving forwards using your seat and legs. Using your rein to turn the horse can set them off-balance, which means they cannot rear.

When it is safe, you should dismount. Rearing horses are not for beginners, and even the most prolific riders may have to seek assistance to fix this problem.

Running Away

Well-trained horses very rarely run away; however, there are sometimes that they will get frightened enough just to run. For example, if a group of children run out of the woods and spook your horse whilst trail riding, you will find that if one horse spooks when it is in company, the others will usually follow suit. If you find that you no longer have control, do your utmost to ride the situation out. When you feel that you can try and regain control of your horse, use your reins and voice. With your reins, the aim is to make the horse turn in a circle and decrease the circles in size until it finally stops.

Backing Up

Significantly few horses will back up when they are not asked to do so because horses do not like going backward, but they are usually trying to resist you when they do. You need to make sure that you are not telling the horse to go backward accidentally, and if you are not and it is the horse that is trying to get out of doing something, you need to make it work.

The best way to do this is to make the horse go back until they do not want to do this anymore. When the horse does not want to keep moving back and when you decide to move forwards, cue the horse to move forward. You will usually find that this does the trick, and the problem is rectified. You may find that you have to spend an entire day going backward, but the horse will learn that they will end up working one way or another!

Backing up is sometimes an indication of evasion behavior that can turn into rearing if not handled and fixed. When a horse feels like they are running backward, use your seat to push them forward and keep your legs wrapped firmly to the horse's sides.

Some Western horses are trained to go back when the rider leans forward. This can be confusing for the horse when an English rider tries to ride them, as they often incline their upper body forward when they cue the horse to walk. Therefore, if you are riding a Western-trained horse and it begins to back up, check your body position and make sure that you are sitting up straight. You may also want to try leaning slightly back to see if this stops the horse from backing up; if it does, then the backing may just have been down to a miscommunication.

Chapter 5 - Ride On

The first thing you need to know when horseback riding is how to mount, or you will never find yourself enjoying the pleasures of horseback riding.

Prepare to Mount

You will be pleased to know that you are not expected to mount a horse as seen in the Western films where the actor takes a flying leap! Mounting is far easier than that, although it can be challenging to haul your entire body weight into the saddle.

Where to Mount

The first thing to determine is where you are going to mount the horse. You need to choose a place where you have plenty of room to get up into the saddle, and this should not be near an open gate or door as this may act as a distraction for your horse, and you could end up falling off before you even get started!

If you have chosen to ride English style, your stirrups will be shorter, which means you will have to raise your leg further to get on. English riders can mount from the ground. However, you may find it easier to use a mounting block; this block is up to 2 feet high and has a couple of steps.

Western riders will also occasionally use a mounting block as it is the easiest way to get on, and it is also better on the horse's back. Mounting from the ground is more manageable when riding

Western style as the stirrups are longer.

Getting on

Riders have spent hundreds of years developing the easiest and safest way to mount a horse, and as such, this has been well established in the horse community, and almost all riders practice it. There are slight differences between how an English rider and a Western rider get on their horses which we will look at now.

Prepare to mount

It is easier to mount using a Western saddle than with an English saddle as Western riders use longer stirrups; a Western saddle is less likely to slip, and there is more saddle to hold you in place. Use the following steps to make mounting easier for you:

1. Lead your horse to the area where you will get on; if you are using a mounting block, put this next to the saddle, approximately one foot from your horse.

2. Take your position and be sure to keep hold of your horse, place the reins over the horse's head, and grip onto the reins. Stand by the horse's left shoulder facing the horse's hindquarters; with your reins in your left hand, grab hold of the front of the saddle.

3. Grasp the stirrup with your right hand and put your left foot into it.

4. Swing yourself up into the saddle.

5. Place your other foot in the stirrup, gather your reins, and you are ready to go!

I always find it helps if you bounce on the spot a couple of times to help launch yourself up; try to use the weight transference rather than pulling on the saddle. Swing your right leg over the horse's hindquarters and avoid touching them before gently sitting on the saddle.

Holding the reins and cues

Depending on the discipline you choose, you have two different ways that you can hold the reins. An English rider will hold the reins in both hands, with enough rein taut to keep in contact with the horse's mouth and give them a little slack in their hands. The Western rider usually holds their reins together in their left hand if their horse is wearing a curb bit and knows how to neck-rein. However, if their horse is in a snaffle bit, the western rider tends to hold the reins the same way as the English rider.

There are a variety of rein cues where your hands and reins work together to form the natural aid of your hands. The best way to look at this is that the reins are an extension of your hands, and your hands complement your legs.

Rein cues

The following are the rein cues that you can use:

Direct rein

This cue keeps the horse straight and prevents it from bending left or right. To carry this cue out, you pull the reins gently back towards your hips.

Indirect rein

The indirect rein cue bends the horse either left or right. If you want to use an indirect

rein to make a right turn, you place your right hand on the horse's withers and move your left hand out and forward so that the horse can bend to the right. Advanced riders' control

the horse's haunches and lateral moves using this technique.

Leading rein

You can use this cue to lead the horse in the direction you want it to go; it is also called open rein. You can then extend your arm out to the side where you want to turn the horse.

Neck rein

Using the neck rein cue puts pressure on one side of the horse's neck. Both of your hands move in the same way to guide the horse. This rein cue is more common in Western riding when using a curb bit and riding with just one hand.

Pulley rein

Pulley rein is also referred to as an emergency rein and uses extreme force in an upward and backward action which forces the horse to stop, but you should only ever use one rein in this way and a true emergency such as loss of control. The horse's head will then turn in towards you and form a circle.

Natural Aids

Now that you can mount your horse, you are ready to set off on your horseback riding future. You will hear about natural aids from day one as these are your primary tools when riding and include your hands, legs, seat, and voice.

Hands

Your hands are an essential way to communicate with your horse, as they hold the direct route to the horse's mouth via the bit and the reins. The way you use your hands directly impacts how well you send signals to the front of your horse, and it is these signals that communicate speed and direction.

The amount of contact your hands have with your horse's mouth depends on the discipline you ride in. For example, in dressage, you keep the reins taut, which gives you direct contact with the bit, whereas, in Western, the reins are looser until you want to stop your horse.

Legs

There are two leading leg positions; the first is "at the girth", and this is where your calf is sitting against the horse behind the edge of the girth, and you use this to bend and drive your horse forwards. The other is known as "behind the girth", where your leg sits about 4" behind at the girth position.

Your legs are also vital in your riding communication tools as you can use them to cue the horse in various things, including direction and speed, and your legs control your horse's hindquarters. The length of stirrups is specific with each discipline, riding style, and which part of your leg has the most contact with the horse.

Your stirrups must be the right length to use your legs correctly. If they are too long, you will not be secure in your seat and use your legs properly. On the other hand, if your stirrups are too short, you will put immense pressure on your ankles and knees, and you could find that you use far too much leg in your communication.

Seat

The seat is important but often forgotten about as a natural aid and method of communication. Using your seat correctly will assist you in getting the horse to move forwards and stop and turn. Your seat equates to your weight and how you move in the saddle. When you want the horse to stop, you sink into the saddle, which tells the horse that you are preparing to stop, preventing the forward motion in the saddle. The horse is then alerted that you need to stop.

You can also use your seat to propel your horse forward by using a gentle push like you would push a book across a table with your bottom. Your seat should always follow the direction of your horse's hindquarters. It is crucial that you sit correctly in the saddle and if you stand up in your stirrups and then sit down and drop your weight down into your heels. You should be able to imagine a straight line running from your ear, through your shoulders, through your hip and to the back of your heel. Your lower back should be flat, and your seat should be able to push forward and downwards.

Many riders perch themselves too far forward in the saddle, which makes them hunch over. You will then be ahead of the horse's motion, causing them to fall forwards when the horse moves. To correct this seat, you need to tighten your stomach muscles, rock your seat bones under the body, lift from your sternum and breathe as deeply as you can.

New riders also tend to sit on a horse as though they are in a reclining chair, however in this position, they are pushing their seat towards the cantle, causing them to raise their thighs and lower legs, and they are then behind the horse's motion.

You need to keep a straight back and pelvis; otherwise, you will be giving wrong cues to your horse, and your shoulders should stay in a parallel position with your horse's shoulder.

While this natural aid can be challenging to understand when you first start riding, you need to know how to use it effectively when you are more advanced.

Voice

The voice is the most direct aid for all novice and beginner riders to grasp, as, through your tone of voice and words, you can communicate many things to your horse, including speeding up or slowing down praise or correction.

You will often need to use your voice and will find yourself asking the horse to walk on, trot and canter. "Whoa" is the verbal command that tells your horse that you want it to slow and stop. Other voice commands include clicking and kissing. Clicking encourages the horse to move quicker, such as from a walk to a trot. The kissing is usually the cue for a horse to canter.

You need to be sensitive with your verbal cues when other horses are around, as other horses may react to you instead of their rider!

Artificial Aids

Many riders use artificial aids as part of their everyday riding equipment, which refers to whips, spurs, etc. Whilst these may sound like torture aids, used correctly, they can help you and your horse to communicate better. Not all horses will require these aids, but there are more that do.

It would be best to have reasonable control before you put on your spurs or clutch your whip and use your hands and legs properly.

Spurs

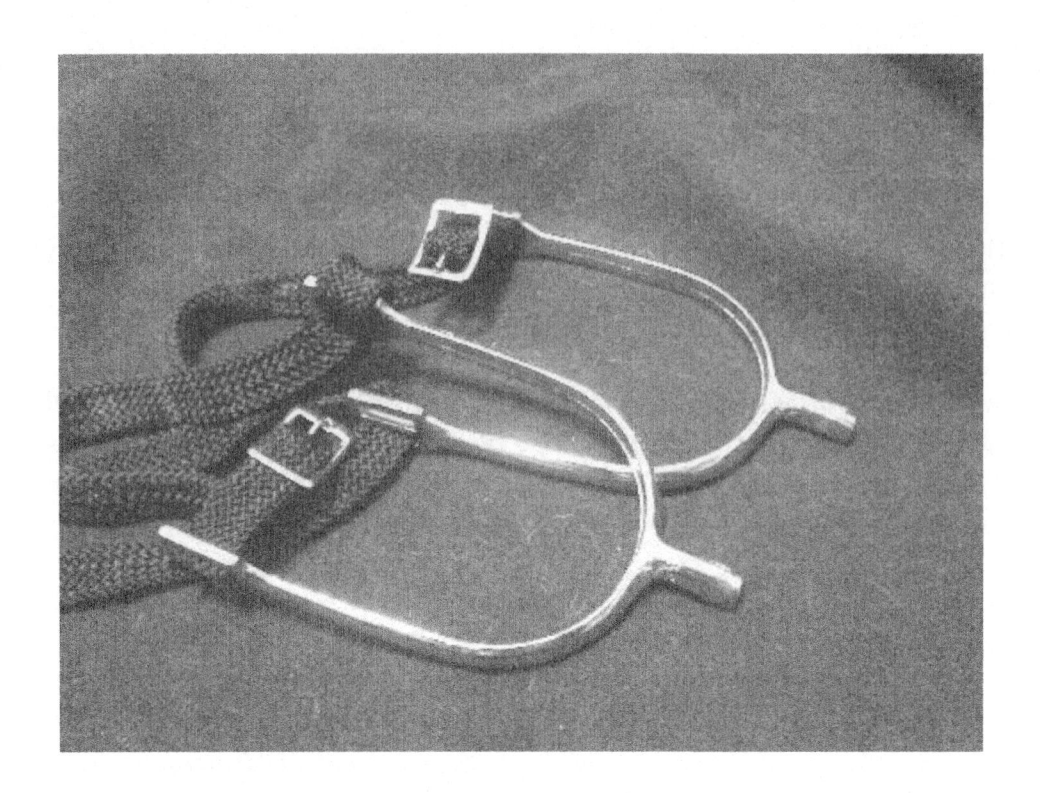

to the girth area with a gentle squeeze.

Spurs are a metal device that fits the rider's heels attached with a leather or nylon strap.
Although English and Western spurs look different, they function in the same way, sending a strong signal to the horse. Once competent enough to use spurs, you apply the spurs

Western spurs

Western spurs are a lot more decorative than English ones,

and they also come in many different styles. Western spurs have a sharp-toothed wheel known as a rowel located at the shank. Some of the milder wheel rowers are smooth, and the type of rowel you decide to use is dependent on

how much contact you want between you and the horse — the sharper the rowel, the stronger the connection. Western spurs are stainless steel, or if you have a deeper pocket, you can have them engraved in silver.

English spurs are simple stainless steel and are devoid of wheels but work in the same way as the Western spurs.

Whips

Many people think of whips as instruments used to punish, but a good rider will never use a whip in this way. The whip provides a different type of communication from rider to horse. If your horse is appropriately trained, a gentle tap on the rear with a whip will send the message, and these messages vary per discipline.

Western and English riders use whips, and the type of whip depends on what you are trying to get the horse to do. The following are the most common style of whips that you will come across:

- **Crop**

Crops are what some riders refer to as sticks or bats and are medium in size that measures between 22" – 27" in length. They feature a leather popper at one end and a hand strap at the other. Due to the size of these whips, they are easy for riders to handle and used by Western and English riders.

- **Fly Whisk**

Western riders favor the fly whisk, and it is usually constructed with a wooden shaft and leather handle with horsehair bristles to the end. The fly whisk measures approximately 21" in length.

- **Dressage**

Dressage whips are longer than crops between 36" – 45" and have a leather hand grip

and capped end with a short lash at the other end.

- **Quirt**

The quirt is a thick braided leather strap that measures approximately 30" and has a looped handle on one end and two additional leather straps on the other. Western riders only use this type of whip.

Chapter 6 - Gaits, Exercising and Training

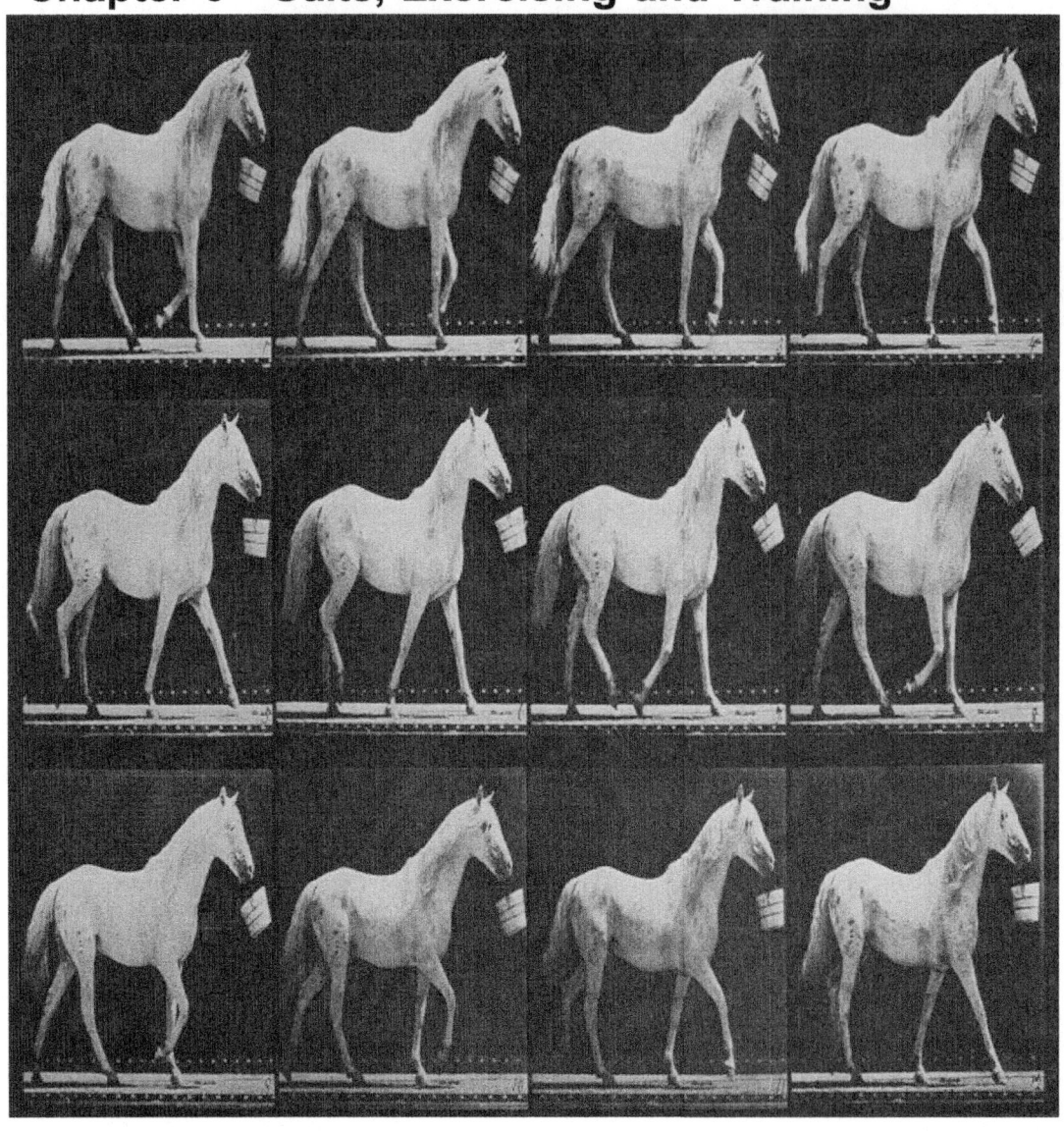

You need to master the first gait, which is walking when you are beginning to learn how to horseback ride. The walk is the slowest gait and at this pace, you have plenty of time to give the horse the correct cues.

When a horse walks it is a rocking, gentle movement which does not rely on the rider for any guidance. When any horse walks, they move in a certain way, they start with their left rear leg, followed by their left front, then their right rear followed by their right front. This sequence always sees horses with three of their legs on the ground.

When you walk in horseback riding it does not matter what discipline you are in, you must establish and maintain the correct body position, and know what to do with your hands and legs as this helps you to communicate with the horse and keep your balance. When you are ready for the horse to walk you give it the cue to move forwards, although the cues can be different for different disciplines, however, they all do have many similarities. Remember that not all horses are the same, you may find one to be very responsive to your cues whilst others need a lot more coaxing. I suggest you start with a quiet cue and if the horse does not respond you can intensify the way you use the cue.

Western cues

When riding Western you need to ensure that your reins are loose then gently squeeze the horse with your calves to ask it to walk. Then you must keep up the pressure until the horse starts to move forwards. Once the horse is walking you can relax your legs. by gently squeezing the horse's sides with your calves. You need to maintain this pressure until the horse moves forward, once the horse responds, relax your leg contact.

English cues

English riders ask their horse to walk using their calves to apply pressure to the horse's sides and this pressure should be maintained until the horse is moving in walk how you want it to and then you can relax your calves, but make sure you do not take the pressure off completely as you should always have a light leg contact with the horse.

When riding in the hunt seat you need to ensure that your reins are not too loose or too tight and you must keep a constant pressure, which runs in a straight line from the horse's bit to your elbow. Alternatively, when doing dressage on a horse you should keep slight tension in your reins as this allows you to keep in close contact with your horse via the bit.

The walk-in Western horseback riding

Western-style horseback riding is comfortable as it is a slow and easy pace for the horse. The walk is the most used pace in Western style when trailing and therefore you need to maintain the right body position. Your reins should be held naturally with your hands just above the horse's withers and your legs still with the balls of your feet secure in the stirrups.

When the horse starts to walk you will feel the movement beneath you and it is this rhythm that you should tune into and become one with the horse. The horse's shoulders will move first left and then right then let your body relax and enjoy the ride.

The walk-in Hunt seat

When riding your horse in a walk using a hunt seat this pace is used to get the horse warmed up and prepared for the faster paces. Horses used for hunt seat riding tend to have larger strides and this can make their walk appear a lot faster. This gait is great for beginners as mastering this walk helps them to maintain good rhythm and balance with the horse.

When you ride in hunt seat you need to use a distinct position in the saddle, stay relaxed and not panic, just relax into the horse and mirror the movement. You should bend your hips and not your waist whilst keeping your weight distributed evenly in the saddle. Your shoulders need to be square, and you should avoid hunching over. Keep your elbows tucked into your body, chin up and look directly ahead.

The Dressage Walk

If you are going to compete in dressage events, then you will find that walk is the most important pace as most maneuvers are carried out at walk. When riding in the dressage discipline you must sit deep into the saddle, your hands should be held just above the withers and your calves sit quietly just behind the girth. When you sit deeply on your bottom and sink into the saddle. Relax your shoulders so that they are square and open, your back flat, chin up, and looking straight ahead.

When you ride the dressage discipline you should make it look effortless. There are many things that can show up when walking a dressage horse and the walk is the easiest pace to spoil and the most difficult to repair particularly if the horse has been forced during its training.

Riding in dressage should look easy and effortless. When you are walking and moving with the horse, there are many faults that can appear. Walk is the easiest gait to ruin and most difficult to repair, this can be because tension has developed due to forced training of the horse.

Trotting

Trotting is performed in a diagonal two-beat gait, this means that two of the horse's feet (diagonals) land on the ground at the same time for a single beat. The horse pushes off and their hooves are suspended in the air for a split second before the other diagonal hooves strike to create the second beat. The sequence for the trot comprises the right hind and left fore (the suspension) followed by the left hind and right fore (the second suspension). It is the suspension which makes the pace feel bumpy, but there should not be any additional beats. The horse's diagonal legs move together, and a good trot should have the hindquarters engaged. When in an extended trot, the suspension will be longer, and in the same way, this moment of suspension can be shorter in a collected trot. The tempo, however, should remain the same whether the trot is extended or collected.

The jog is a shortened, relaxed trot that features minimum suspension, which is more likely to be seen in Western horse competition, and this is a comfortable gait for both the horse and rider over long distances.

In the same way as walking, the trot can have various faults such as being stiff and hollow, this causes the muscles on the hindquarters to tense, and the horse will not have the natural swinging motion, which then causes a rough trot which is challenging to ride. The trot can also lose suspension, meaning that the horse loses its spring. This is mainly seen in Western horses that can jog incredibly slowly.

The trot can also have a false extension, so when the horse moves forwards, its toe flips up, and the horse exaggeratedly hyperextends its forelegs. The horse stretches its legs to cover more ground with the front legs, but they do not have enough power to push onwards; this is called toe-flipping or goose-stepping.

Diagonals and Posting

If you ride English, you will probably post your trot, and this is the up and down movement that makes the trot more comfortable. The movement is a forward and backward movement where the rider rocks their hips back and forward using the horse for their push for the upward movement. Beginners rise up and down as this is easy to understand. Sitting trot can be difficult for English riders, and they will usually post; however, dressage riders spend most of their time executing sitting trot once they have warmed the horse up using the posting trot.

The rider sits and rises with one diagonal pair of legs. If the rider posts with the left front leg and the right hind, the rider posts on the left diagonal. It is customary for the rider to post on the outside diagonal apart from riding dressage in America. They then switch their diagonals when asking the horse for more engagement of the hind legs. For example: when you are riding to the right, you are on the left diagonal, and when you change direction, you should also switch diagonals.

New riders can find diagonals a bit of a mystery; however, if you remember this rhyme, you will always be right, "Rise and fall with the leg on the wall". In other words, look down at your horse's shoulder, and when you see the horse's right front leg move forward, you should rise in your stirrups, and when it moves back, you sit back again. You may find that it takes a few strides to get into the proper swing, and then when you switch directions, you need to think and sit for a beat and resume posting. If you find you are not on the correct diagonal, you can sit for a couple more beats and then rise. That should see you on the right track again. It is common to find that you can post better in one direction than the other.

Switching your diagonals a few times whilst looking down at your horse's shoulder, you will gradually start to feel what posting on the correct diagonal feels like and how rough the ride can feel if you are on the wrong one. To get the hang of posting, you should practice on the same horse as horse's trots vary in rhythm and bounce.

Cantering

The canter is a three-beat gait with suspension. The sequence for the canter is:

- Outside hind leg (First beat)

- Diagonal pair of legs (Second beat)

- Inside Foreleg (Third beat)

- Suspension

When a horse canters, the leg leads the motion. The sequence for the left lead is:

- Right hind leg

- Left hand and right fore (diagonal pair)

- Left fore or leading foreleg (suspension)

The sequence for the right lead is:

- Left hind leg

- Right hind and right fore (diagonal pair)

- Right fore or leading foreleg (suspension)

The horse will typically lead with the inside leg, so if you are cantering to the left, the left foreleg should be leading and vice versa with the right. If you are cantering with the outside leg, it can make it hard to turn, and this is often called the wrong leg or false lead.

When a horse turns and changes the leading leg, this is known as a lead change. A horse can change leads if they are performing a flying lead change within one canter stride. Horses can also achieve a simple lead change by breaking into a trot and changing leads as they move forwards again in canter. A good canter should be light, regular, and active. Cantering is more collected than the gallop, and the gait is a rocking motion that is easy for the rider to stay seated and one of the most lovely gaits for the rider.

The lope is an unconstrained, relaxed canter performed with the rider having a loose rein, and the horse is still in a three-beat canter with suspension. This horse may have a long frame, and they carry their neck lower with less suspension. Typically, this is a Western version of the canter.

When cantering, the horse should remain supple with good coordination and balance. Sometimes horses can get confused by a cue to canter, which sees them strike on the wrong leg. Other mistakes horses can make in canter are a fumbled departure into canter or change of leads because they are not balanced. Cross-firing is when the horse switches their lead multiple times whilst moving in the same direction. Cross-canter should not be confused with cross-firing as the cross-canter is when the horse is on one lead with the hind legs and the other lead with its forelegs.

Galloping

The gallop is a four-beat gait with suspension. The gait is also a set of jumps and is the horse's natural running gait. Horses gallop when they are frightened, or they need to get somewhere very quickly. Riders rarely gallop; the fastest they get is an extended canter. The gallop sequence is like the canter apart for the inside hind leg lands first instead of diagonal pairs landing together.

The gallop sequence is:

- Outside hind leg

- Inside hind

- Outside foreleg

- Inside (leading) foreleg

(suspension) The left lead gallop sequence is:

- Right hind

- Left hind

- Right fore

- Left fore (leading foreleg) (suspension)

The right lead gallop sequence is:

- Left hind

- Right hind

- Left fore

- Right fore (leading foreleg) (suspension)

The gallop is an extended gait with long strides, and to help the horse engage its hind legs for each stride, it will use its abdominal muscles. The horse's head and neck oscillate forward and back to keep them balanced. The horse draws a breath with each stride, and the speed of the gallop varies from horse to horse.

The hand gallop is a controlled gallop where the gait should be well-balanced so the horse can handle any direction changes and changes in the ground. This is used in show jumping and sometimes in the show ring. There are faults in the gallop like those in canter; a gallop can be disjointed and on the wrong lead. Horses can also scramble in the gallop, but this is generally racers or showjumpers up against the clock.

Backing up

Some horses are more scared of backing up as this is

something that does not come naturally. If a horse needs to go back from where they have come from, it will usually turn around rather than back up. In some cases, they may feel trapped and back up. Going backward does not come naturally to a horse, as they must move around in a diagonal pattern. Backing up is a four-beat maneuver. The sequence of a backup is:

- Right fore

- Left hind

- Left fore

- Right hind

Horses should turn back in a calm and collected manner, flexing at the poll and mouth, and should willingly move forwards when asked. Horses should not drag their feet when asked to move backward.

Transitions

When you change from one gait to another or from a halt, a transition occurs. Horses make transitions automatically and quickly on their own; however, you need to prompt them using cues when you are riding them. Some riders will encourage their horse by using a clicking noise for trot and again for canter.

Horses will make their transitions gradually when they are in the field without their rider. They will move from a standstill to walk, then trot, then canter, and do this in reverse when they slow down. When ridden, though, horses may miss a gait and go from walk to canter. They also go from halt to trot, but it is more usual for a horse to walk a few steps before moving onto trot. Horses that skip gaits are generally supple and balanced.

For beginner riders, it is natural to use the horse's natural way of transitioning, and then as they become more at home with the gaits, they can learn how to skip gaits. To execute a smooth transition, it is the rider that should prepare the horse for the transition. They do this by proving the right aids and timed right; the rider will remain balanced with the horse, and the gait changes. If the rider is off-balance and tips forwards or backward, the horse will become upset and be unable to transition cleanly, and the rider will have to use their natural feel and balance so that they can feel when the horse is ready to start transitions.

Exercise & Training Regimes

One of your main aims as a new horseback rider is to get your horse used to you and listen to you. When horseback riding, it is essential that you keep your horse ready for your command and that they are not looking around trying to find something else to interest them. The best way to achieve this is to change your routine regularly and do some suppling exercises. These will release any stiffness in the horse, similar to stretching exercises that you may do yourself.

The question is, "How can you do this?" For starters, do not just wander around walking lap after lap, then mirror this in trot, without adding anything to get your horse to listen to you and pay attention. There are many ways to practice this, one is by incorporating gait transitions, and the other is to ride patterns.

Gait Transitions

I have always found that it is ideal to start with gait transitions. It is best to start at a walk as your horse will need to warm up. While walking, you get the idea of how sensitive your horse is by asking every couple of strides to halt. To ask for a halt, you need to sit deep into your saddle, so your horse feels the weight and gently bring the reins back towards your stomach as soon as the horse halts; immediately put your hands forward, so there is no cross-communication with the horse as it has obeyed your command.

Practicing gait transactions is the perfect way for you and your horse to get a feel for each other. Gait transactions are when you change your gait, such as going from walk to trot or canter to walk. By asking your horse to change pace multiple times, you will keep the horse alert and awaiting your next instruction. You can apply the gait transitions in accordance with your own experience.

Patterns

One of the most straightforward patterns to carry out is the circle. Once you are ready to walk, squeeze your calves around the horse and ask it to move forwards. Once you have a good pace, walk a couple of strides, and turn your horse in a big circle (25 meters). Apply a little more leg as you start to turn, as many horses tend to slow down when turning in a circle. Circling is an excellent way to get your horse supple while warming up; it will keep your horse's attention. Complete one circle, then continue walking until you are ready to repeat the circle or move on to something else.

When you circle, the circle should be round, and the horse should be on the arc of the circle with its body bent into the turn. To ride a good circle, you should apply your legs behind the girth so that you push the horse's rib cage round into its backbone. You may also want to use a light squeeze on your inside rein to get the horse's nose turned in slightly. If you turn your head towards the center of your circle, you should be able to see in your peripheral vision the corner of your horse's eye and the point of his hip, this way, you know that you have a good bend through the horse's back.

Once you have mastered the circle, there are various other patterns you can create with your horse, such as:

1. Figure of 8

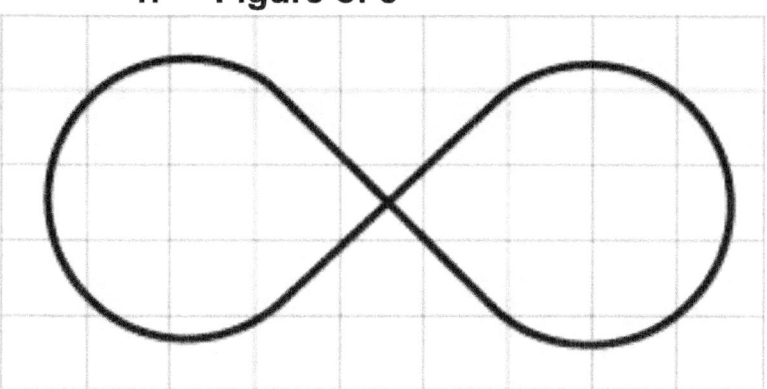

Begin by walking in a large circle. As you finish the process (getting back to where you started), prepare to go the other way and create another circle in the opposite direction next to the first circle, keeping both circles the same shape and size. Apply your legs as you did in the circle, so your circle on the figure of 8 is well rounded. As you come across the center to change direction, ride the horse straight for two strides, then change the bend. Once you have mastered this pattern, you can incorporate gait transitions such as halting in the middle between the two circles when you have created the figure of 8.

2. Spirals

Begin by walking in a circle and expanding the size of the circle by thinking of the circle with multiple rings that create tracks, and you will ride your horse on these tracks. To ride on the outer track, sit and drop your weight onto your outside seat bone and push your horse on using your inside leg, and you will feel the horse move over. Hold onto the imaginary track as you block further movement to the outer rings with your outside leg and by shifting your weight back to the center of your saddle. Next, take your horse to create an inner circle, sit into your inside stirrup, put your weight on your inside seat bone and push through your outside leg. Hold your horse to the inner track using your inside leg and sit squarely in the saddle again.

3. Serpentine

A serpentine is created with big loops where you ask your horse to change direction across the area every time you reach the outer edge. You can create a serpentine with 3 or 4 equal loops. Riding a serpentine is easy, and you need to turn the horse from the short side down the long side of your work area, crossing the center of the area, then riding straight directly across the other long side and then change direction down the long side. Ride for a few strides, look across the area and ride across the center again towards the other long side. When you get to the side, change direction again and ride a few more strides, look across to the other long side, turn through the center, and head towards the other long side, switching the direction as you get to it.

It would help if you kept in mind the following when you are creating the serpentine. Firstly, you need to keep the horse balanced and do not allow it to fall at each turn, and you can achieve this by sitting square in the saddle then transferring your weight for the direction you wish to turn in.) Secondly, ride straight across the area parts of the serpentine as straight as you can. When you turn, find a spot on the area to ride to which is straight across from you and ride straight at it using your leg and seat. In both cases, you also need to apply the bending aids whenever you turn.

4. Simple Serpentine

To create a simple serpentine, you need to ride from the long side of your area to the quarter line. As you finish your turn from the short side to the long side, ride your horse on a diagonal bend toward the inside quarter line. Once you get to the quarter line, ride your horse for a stride, change the bend, so he bends to the area outer edge and then moves on the diagonal back to the outer edge. Straighten the horse for a stride, then change the bend towards the inside, ride the horse to the quarter line and repeat. This exercise is the perfect way to get a horse nice and supple.

5. Volte and Reverse

To ride a volte and reverse is like riding a teardrop shape. You start by riding down the long side of your area and begin turning in as if you are turning a small circle but instead ride back to the outer edge, then go the other way. In this exercise, you need to keep the loop rounded and leg yield back to the rail.

6. Leg Yield – (Side pass in western)

When undertaking a leg yield, you ask the horse to move forwards and across so that the horse crosses its legs over one another using your seat and leg aid. In the English riding discipline, leg yield is referred to as a lateral movement due to how the horse moves. To carry out a leg yield, as you ride down the short side of the area heading to the long side, turn in early so that you are on the area's quarter line (about 5 feet away from the edge). Ride the quarter line straight, then step into your outside stirrup and apply your inside leg in an on-off command; continue with this leg action, and you should feel the horse step over, across, and forward, ride this leg yield until you reach the other side.

All the six patterns above will help you and your horse listen to one another, and this will also teach you how to ride in a straight line, through transitions, and achieve the correct bend to keep the horse's hindquarters and back supple. Carrying out the patterns will help you develop your coordination and balance, which will help you to become a better rider. The riding gait transitions, and lateral movements strengthen the horse, particularly in the back legs and hindquarters.

If you are riding a nervous horse, riding patterns can help the horse to feel less anxious and get used to different environments. The horse must think about what they are being asked to do and have no time to worry; this is also an excellent way to ensure that it is using its body correctly.

Once you have mastered the patterns in the walk, you can move on to carry them out in a trot, and you can also incorporate gait transitions within the patterns.

When you are riding a horse, whether you are making circles, patterns, gait transactions, or any other type of exercise, you must remember how sensitive your horse is, even if it does not show. Think about how a horse reacts to an annoying fly buzzing around its legs; the horse swishes its tail, kicks up a leg, and does everything to try and remove the fly. Therefore, if you feel that your horse is not sensitive to your aids, think again! Being sensitive is natural for a horse and makes perfect sense because when horses are in the wild, and they are not sensitive, the chances are that they would end up as someone else's dinner!

We have taken the horse from its natural environment to live with humans; if this horse is with a human, that repeatedly exposes it to incorrect/conflicting aids. The best way to explain this is if you were to apply your leg and pull back on the reins simultaneously. When horses are subjected to this type of stimuli, they will eventually shut down their awareness of the area. The horse will then tune out to your aids and become challenging to get moving, requiring you to kick and cluck and even a few taps of the whip to get any response.

The way to ensure that your horse does not become desensitized is to work hard on riding correctly and keeping your riding aids distinctive and steady. Desensitization can also occur when the rider does not give the horse sufficient praise and rewards for completing things accurately. The term "rewards" does not mean pony nuts or carrots or even lots of pats on its neck (although these are always good); the best way you can reward your horse is to end its work for the day by completing its work. The horse will know it has done well and has earned a reward for it.

If a horse is asked to perform the same exercises repeatedly, even when it is doing everything correctly, it can eventually become desensitized, and the worst case grows sour. Who can blame it, though? The horse is doing its best to please you, but you keep making it repeat everything, so it does not know when it has done everything correctly. When riding a horse, you are constantly training them, even if you are a new rider with little experience. You are telling the horse what it must do when you ask it to and what you will not tolerate; therefore, no matter how inexperienced you are, the horse will still learn from you both the good and the bad that you are teaching it.

Chapter 7 – Jumping

When you soar over a fence on horseback, the feeling you get is exhilarating and like nothing else. Jumping is not part of dressage or Western disciplines, however for jump seat riders, this is the goal, and once you jump, it is difficult not to fall in love. However, it is worth mentioning that jumping is not for everyone, and there is so much else you can achieve with a horse that you should not make it your be-all and end-all.

Safety is an essential issue, particularly when you start learning to jump. To begin with, you should never attempt jumping unless your teacher is with you, and you must always wear an approved safety hat and body protector. Your instructor should also start you off on an experienced horse known for its capabilities to jump with a total novice on its back.

Different types of jumping

Jumping is an exciting part of riding in the schooling area; however, jumping in a competition is even more of a rush. Hunt seat riders work towards eventually jumping in one of the many competitions that are available to them. Each competition offers a variety of challenges and requires a particular type of horse and rider. There is no reason you cannot jump just for fun; however, many riders go on to compete once they have learned to jump.

Jumping in an Arena

Most jumping competitions take place in an outdoor ring or an indoor arena. Riders can either compete in show jumping or hunters.

Showjumping

If you have ever watched televised equestrian

classes, you will probably have seen the sport that is referred to in the equestrian world as showjumping. Regardless of the venue, the rules are the same. The only difference is the skill level and experience of both horse and rider and prize money.

In showjumping, horses and riders negotiate a course of jumps in a specified time or against the clock and the one that finishes with the fewest faults and or quickest time takes first place. The faults come when a fence is knocked down by the horse, the horse refuses to jump or the rider gets lost and forgets the order they should be jumping the fences in. Other showjumping classes see riders that jump a clear round with no faults going forwards to a jump-off against the clock where the quickest clear round is the winner.

Beginners show jumping is often 2 feet and below, whereas fences for the most experienced riders can top 7 feet.

Hunters

The hunter was named so as it was based on the traditional English sport of fox hunting (although this is now illegal), hunter classes see horse and rider jump a set course in a specific order.

Where show jumping is timed, hunter classes have a judge who scores the horse for its manners and how it looks when it jumps. The fences are lower, standing no higher than 4 feet. Beginners' classes for hunters start with cross rail jumps that can be as low as 12 inches.

There is a dress code for hunter classes, and horses must be groomed in a certain way. Hunter horse's manes are plaited, tails thoroughly brushed, and coat as glossy as possible.

Cross-country jumping

The best way to describe cross-country jumpers is the daredevils of the jumping discipline. Horse and rider jump almost anything that gets in their way! There are cross-country courses for all levels of riders.

Cross-country can also be one of the elements in a three-day event competition where the rider and horse tackle dressage, cross-country, and show jumping over three days, or cross-country can be a stand-alone event. Cross country competitions take place outside, and there are several jumps that span several miles, with the level of the competition determining how many jumps there are and how long the course is. Unlike show jumping where the fences are not solid, cross-country fences are fixed and cannot be knocked down therefore cross-country is a more considerable risk than showjumping.

Cross-country jumps have various objects such as ditches, telephone poles, and water jumps that they need to jump over and or into. The course must be completed over a specific timescale, and as well as time faults, the horse and rider get faults for refusing the jump or the rider falling off.

The jumps on a cross-country course can start with a pole on the ground and move to ditches that measure 11 feet with a drop so when the horse lands they are lower than where they took off. As cross-country fences vary so much, there will be some long jumps and tall ones, which means the horse must jump further rather than higher.

Types of fences

If you are planning to learn how to jump, you need to recognize the type of fences you could come across. Each fence is different and offers challenges and learning experiences for both horse and rider. Instructors always start their students on easy jumps, to begin with, and then when they are ready, they progress onto the higher and more challenging fences.

Cross rail's/Cross Pole

The Cross rail or Cross pole, which the English use as a warmup fence, is the first jump beginners start on. Cross rail's/Cross poles are made using two poles that create an X shape between two stands. This jump is designed so that horses can get used to jumping in the center and to encourage them with their jumping. This is also the best fence for beginners as it teaches them to look for the middle of the fence. The mistake beginners make with this fence is not aiming the horse in the center of the X.

Verticals

More advanced than the Cross rail or Cross pole is the vertical fence, but it is still a suitable jump for beginners. Vertical fences have two jump stands, one on each side with single or double poles fitted onto them horizontally like split rail fencing.

Vertical fences are a great training aid for the rider, as they determine how to judge the required distance for the horse to jump from. New riders find vertical jumps more challenging than Cross rail or Cross poles because the vertical does not give the horse the visual definition. The horse can find it hard to determine when to jump, so it is down to the rider to provide guidance. This can be extremely difficult for new jumpers as they are also judging the distance. The result could see the horse take off at the wrong moment and they may not clear the fence.

Oxers

Oxers are more advanced than vertical fences in verticals as they are more of a three- dimensional obstacle for the horse to negotiate. Oxers are made using two sets of two jump stands and two horizontal poles, making them a deeper jump than a vertical. Oxers can have horizontal poles together, or uneven oxers have the front pole lower than the one behind.

Those new to jumping would not negotiate oxers until they are au fait with Crossrail or Cross poles and verticals and the distances. This is because the horse must jump both width and height with an oxer. This jump teaches horse and rider where they need to take off with the added dimension, getting the pair to estimate distances more accurately.

Walls

One of the most intimidating fences is the wall as they look as though they are solid and look more prominent. A wall is precisely that and stands between jump stands, but rather than bricks and mortar, the wall is created using a set of light blocks that stand on each other and will fall if the horse hits them.

You need a confident horse to jump a wall, one who is not frightened by any type of jump as a wall appears to be more difficult and the horse can be scared as they cannot see what is on the other side.

Cross-country jumps

When starting to jump cross-country fences, riders are faced with relatively easy jumps compared to those experienced riders. The jumps can be anything from poles to shallow plants, from small verticals and oxers.

Jumping cross-country fences will test the stamina of both horse and rider. Riders are expected to use the skills they have learned in the arena to the test in the wide-open space.

The Jumping Process

There are so many reasons horses are such amazing creatures, with their ability to jump being just one of them. Horses can jump and this seems to come naturally to them, however, they do need to be taught the correct technique. Horses must have good form (the way they carry themselves) over the fences, be obedient for the rider and have the courage (it takes a lot to jump without knowing where they may land and facing some intimidating obstacles too.)

The 2-point position

Prior to jumping, you must know how your body should be placed when your horse takes off over a jump. Known as the 2-point, this position helps the rider to keep their balance when they lift off, of the horse's back to help them clear the jump. It would be best if you practiced the 2-point position before doing any jumping. Practicing the position regularly will help you build the muscles in your legs to hold yourself easily in the 2-point position throughout the jumps.

The following is how to hold your two-point position in one motion:

- Bend forwards from your hips so your chest is at a 45-degree angle with the

   horse's body.

- Put your weight down into your heels and keep your knees in contact with the saddle without squeezing.

- Lift yourself off the saddle but not wholly.

- Your hands should be low, on the horse's neck.

- Keep your head up, looking straight ahead.

Time to Jump

I know you probably think that this is all well and good, but how can you get a horse to jump? Simply, aim it towards the fence, push them forward with your legs and they should jump!

As a rider, your job is to:

- Keep the horse in the center

- Control the horse's speed, so the approach to the jump is controlled

- Assume the correct body position and allow the horse to jump without you interfering

The horse will do the rest!

When you jump fences one after another, you must measure how the horse strides and check their speed, so they take off at the right place. Some horses can figure the distances themselves but as the rider, it is your job to guide the horse.

Before jumping, your horse should be warmed up; you should walk and trot for at least 10 minutes so that the horse is supple and ready to work.

Once you are ready to jump, follow the steps below:

1. Trot – make sure you are happy with your horse's speed and feel comfortable and balanced. Turn toward the fence, ensure you have adequate distance between you and the jump on the approach.
2. Keep your legs squeezing on the approach to the jump and aim at the center of the jump. You will probably find that the horse pricks its ears as it anticipates the jump. Make sure to keep looking where

you are going, as looking down could send you off balance.
3. Once you are a couple of strides from the jump, assume the 2-point position and remember to keep both legs pushing the horse forward.
4. As your horse jumps, hold the 2-point position, and mentally prepare yourself to land.
5. Once the horse reaches the floor, stay in the 2-point position for two strides, then lower yourself back into the saddle.

Multiple jumps

Once you have mastered one jump, your teacher may let you begin jumping multiple jumps. Different multiple-jump patterns are a great way for you to learn and master certain jump skills. Your teacher can then watch you over a series of jumps and provide you with their feedback.

Grid

Probably the first jump pattern you will come across is the grid, and this is designed to teach you how to remain balanced when jumping, and the grid is made up of 2 – 4 jumps or poles on the ground. Grid jumps are straightforward, such as Crossrail or Cross poles.

The grid pattern is formed to create measured strides between jumps. When the strides are not measured, a horse may find it hard to know when they should jump; this is a joint effort between horse and rider as the rider needs to help the horse by ensuring the horse is striding right between the jumps.

Premeasured strides make it easy for riders to jump multiple fences. This way, the rider does not have to decipher the number of strides the horse must take between each jump.

Keep inline

Apart from the grid, another basic fence pattern for beginners is a line. Here you have a row of 2 – 3 jumps, these are often Crossrail's/ cross poles with undetermined strides between them. The jumps have not been designed for the horse to take a predetermined number of strides between them; in other words, one fence may have three strides while another could have five.

Here, the rider must determine how many strides the horse takes, and the speed needed to get over the jumps successfully. The rider must communicate this information to the horse by shortening or lengthening its strides accordingly.

Estimating successfully comes with plenty of practice and guidance from your teacher.

On Course

When a novice rider is ready, they are introduced to a course. A course is made up of 7 – 9 different fences. The challenge when riding a jumping course is to keep a forward rhythm. Riders should judge the strides to a fence and control the horse to ensure they take them.

Jumping Issues

Even though it is natural for horses to jump, being asked to jump an array of separate obstacles with a rider when they could easily go around is not. Jumping issues do arise, most of which are man-made, meaning horses develop the problems because of an awful experience brought on by poor riding.

As a beginner, you should not have to deal with the issues as most schoolmasters (teaching horses), which beginners are taught to jump on, are masters and will jump whatever they are asked to. However, if you need to deal with a horse that has jumping issues you need exactly how to tackle them and successfully assist the horse too.

- **Hurrying**

When a horse hurtles towards a jump, they approach too quickly and can then misjudge the take-off and misjudge the correct strides it needs between fences and the horse can end up knocking the fence down.

The cause for a horse to rush at a jump can come from a multitude of things. Sometimes the rider is egging the horse on without noticing, so the horse gets over excited; however, horses can rush because they are anxious. The only way to clear the jump is with plenty of speed, or it could be that the horse will not listen to the rider.

To preschool a horse that rushes, you need to keep a little pressure on your reins but not, so they are taut on approach to the fence. Trot at the jump, jump it and stop. Continue doing this until the horse understands jumping does not have to be flat out. The grid exercise can be helpful if you need to teach the horse patience, and as the jumps come one after another, the horse is forced to slow down.

- **Running away**

Running away sees the horse swerve round the jump rather than jumping it. This type of refusal is usually due to a lack of confidence from both horse and rider. When a horse runs away it can be frightening for the rider as they can be thrown off balance when they are least expecting it.

To get a horse out of the habit of running out you can make a "funnel" using two poles that you lay at either side of the jump stands as this creates a visual presence to assist the horse and keep it straight over the fence and not around it. When you are approaching the jump keep your reins a little shorter and use your seat and your legs to give the horse the confidence it needs to get to the other side.

- **Refusing**

When a horse will not go over a jump, it is refusing! This problem occurs when the horse slams on the brakes just as it should be taking off.

The consequences when a horse will not go over a jump is not pleasant for the rider as they anticipate the horse's going forwards and are thrown off balance. The rider may land on the neck; in the worst case, you end up on the floor.

Horses refuse fences because they are afraid that they cannot make the jump and it is their lack of confidence that makes them stop! Sometimes the issue is that the horse can sense uncertainty with the rider and becomes uncertain too.

You should never punish a horse for refusing to jump; instead, lower the jump and try again, and it could be that you must put the jump on the floor so the horse can walk over it; remember, this is all about rebuilding the horse's confidence.

Chapter 8 – When you finish your ride

When you have finished riding for the day, you need to get off your horse. There are various other things you also need to do before you can pat your horse and leave it for the night. For the sake of your horse, you must not neglect these final tasks, or you may find your horse is reluctant to work for you.

Dismounting

You will be relieved to hear that getting off your horse is not as difficult as getting on. There are two ways to dismount, and one may be easier than the other depending on the size of your horse. Below you will see a brief overview of both:

1. Make sure your horse has stopped. You should never try to dismount if your horse is moving because you could spook the horse if you do.

2. Take your right foot out of the stirrup and hold the front (pommel) if you have an English saddle or (horn) if you have a western saddle with your left hand. Be sure to keep hold of the reins.

3. Swing your right leg over the horse then move your left hand so it is holding the cantle.

4. Lean into the saddle, kick your left foot out of the stirrup, and slide to the ground.

5. Alternatively – for English riders while you are still in the saddle, remove both feet from your stirrups, lean forwards, press your hands into the neck of your horse, bring over your right leg, and slide to the ground.

6. I would not recommend leaving your left foot in the stirrup because if your horse spooks or runs off you are stuck in the stirrup.

For safety reasons ensure that you keep a good hold on your reins.

Untacking your horse

Usually, when a horse has finished its work for the day, they are desperate to get their bridle off. For this reason, this is where you should start. Put the halter (head collar) around the horse's neck, then unbuckle the throat lash and the noseband if you have one.

Gently remove the bridle from the horse's ears, and the horse will probably assist by

spitting out the bit! Then put the head collar on the horse.

The next thing is to remove your English or western girth. When you remove an English girth, you need to undo the left side then the right side. If you have a western saddle, you unloop the latigo then loop and tuck it around the D-ring on the saddle. Go to the right- hand side and lie the girth on the seat of the saddle.

Remove the saddle from the left side of your horse, be sure to lift the saddle and saddle cloth at the same time and put the saddle on a saddle rack or where it is kept. Put the saddle cloth wet side up on top of your saddle so that it can dry out. For an English saddle, you should also make sure to lay the girth over the saddle wet side up so that this can also dry.

Cool your horse down

After a hard ride, horses, like humans, need at least 15 minutes walking to cool down, this depends on the amount of work they have done and the temperature. You can do this either before you get off or walk on a lead rope after you have untacked the horse. The reason for the cooldown is to lower the horse's heart and respiration rate and to completely relax their muscles. As a guide, you should walk the horse as soon as it stops blowing and the flanks are calm, and their neck is cool to touch. If the horse has visible sweat this should be dry and breathing returned to normal. If it is hot, you may give the horse a sponge to cool it down.

It is important not to let the horse eat or drink until it is totally relaxed as this could lead to colic.

Grooming after riding

Typically, horses are clean after a ride, but there are a few things that you can do to ensure it is as comfortable as possible. If your horse has got sweaty you can sponge it down and then use a sweat scraper to scrape off any excess water as this will help to dry them quicker.

Next, you should pick out their feet so that you can remove any clods of mud or rocks that they could have picked up whilst out on the ride. You also need to give your horse a good brush with a soft brush just so the hair is lying flat, and any dust is removed.

Your horse has been good enough to give you the opportunity to enjoy horseback riding, so it seems only fair that you make it as comfortable as possible afterward. Good comparisons are to think how good you feel when you have been to a hairdresser or for a massage, and it is these feelings you are transferring to your horse by washing (if necessary) and brushing them down after your ride. Just spend that extra few minutes, it will help you to create a deeper bond with your horse too.

Chapter 9 - Equestrian Etiquette and Games

Riders are expected to behave in a certain way when they are out on their horse, this really is a dignified hobby. Most of the behaviors are safety-related but they will also hold you in good stead with your fellow equestrians.

Red Ribbon

If your horse has a tendency to kick out whether you are riding with a group or alone the universal signal is to tie a red ribbon around your horse's tail. This tells others to keep their distance. Obviously, if you see a horse wearing a red ribbon you should keep at least one-horse length between you.

Slow and Steady

You see the cowboys in the movies that leap onto their horses and gallop off into the sunset. However, in the real world, equestrians do not behave in this way unless they want to put their horse in danger and annoy everyone that is anywhere near you. For these reasons when you first get on your horse, walk slowly to your destination whether this is a local track or riding arena. Do not trot or canter through your stables or stress your horse by tearing off from a standstill to gallop. This is not the behavior of a sensible rider and puts your horse and others in extreme danger.

Communication is Key

It is important to remember that all riders have different skills and confidence levels with trail riding being possibly the most challenging, for less skilled riders. Therefore, you should always check with fellow riders to make sure everyone feels secure. Do not speed up without ensuring your group is all good to go.

If you are riding in an arena, you also need to communicate with those around you. This is vital if you are planning to jump, be sure that others sharing the arena are good with this, after all, any young horses may spook and become rather unruly as a consequence of your actions.

There is no need to Shout

Shouting and hollering may be fine in cowboy movies but in real life, this is the type of thing that frightens horses, annoys others, and makes you look just plain stupid! The only exception to this is when you are competing at a gymkhana or speed event where these types of vocalizations are acceptable as they are seen as a method to make your horse go faster.

Keep Your Distance

The rule of thumb between equestrians is to keep your horse when riding in a group one- length distance from the horse in front of you. Granted there are times when this can be incredibly difficult as many horses prefer to travel closely together. However, there will be issues if the horse in front suddenly stops and your horse then crashes into it, which could lead to the horse in front kicking out at your horse.

This can be avoided by ensuring that you teach your horse to obey your cues, you should then be able to slow your horse down if it gets too close to the horse in front, creating a safe distance between the two of you. If you find that a rider is following too close to your horse, then ask whether they would like to pass and if not suggest that they may want to circle to ensure the right distance is kept between you.

Approach with Caution

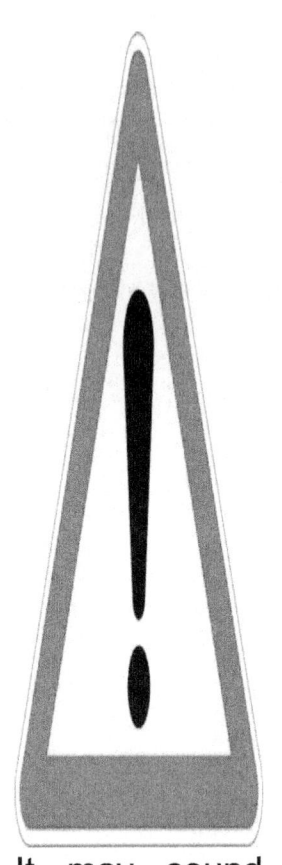

It may sound stupid but if you are approaching a horse from the rear do not run your horse up behind them, if you do there is a likelihood that the horse could spook or take off which may result in a serious accident.

If you are trotting or cantering and need to pass a rider from the rear whilst they are walking, give them a wide berth, this is also applicable if you are trail riding. Even if you slow to a walk, you should let the rider know that you are there, running up behind another horse is a sure way to cause trouble.

Left Shoulder to Shoulder

When you are riding in an arena you will find that you are moving in one direction whilst there are one or more riders traveling in the opposite way. When you pass other riders in an arena, the left shoulder to left shoulder rule should be adhered to. Therefore, when riders pass one another in opposite directions their left shoulders pass each other. This is the equestrian equivalent of driving on the right side of the road in a vehicle. To undertake this, you may find that you need to stay close to the rail so that the approaching rider can pass on your left, or you may find that you need to stay inside away from the rail to have the approaching rider pass you on your left.

There is a good way to remember this rule, this is if you are moving counter clockwise you should stay along the rail if another rider is coming towards you. However, if you are traveling clockwise, you will need to pass the rider on the inside of the arena, allowing them to stay on the rail.

Prepare for Trail Riding

Prior to taking an inexperienced horse out on trails with others, make sure that it is perfectly safe to do so. You should expose your horse to as much as you may come across such as water crossings, tractors, traffic, train tracks, and so on.

If your horse is nervous and easily spooked, let the others in your riding group know so that they can decide if they want to ride with you. Some horses actually pick up on nervous energy from other horses and can then be unruly themselves. This type of havoc can ruin the ride for everyone.

Time for a Drink

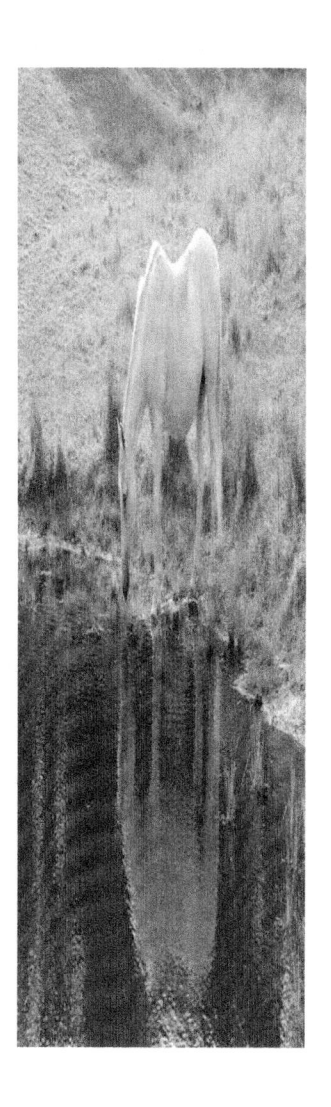

When you are out on a trail with others and you come across a water source, if their horses want to drink then it is only right to stop. Be courteous and wait your turn particularly if the source is too small for one or two horses.

Drinking along a trail is important for your horse particularly when you are on long rides, and you should never discourage fellow riders' horses from drinking. Try to keep your horse quiet and if you are having trouble getting your horse to behave, walk them to one side and wait until the other horses have all had a drink then let your horse have its share. Once all the horses have finished drinking you can set off on your journey again.

Help

Regardless of where you are riding it is vital that you stay aware of other riders. Whilst riding in an arena if you see another rider fall off or their horse bolt stop immediately and wait until the other horse has been brought under control and the rider is checked over too. If you are the only other person around, dismount, and if need be, call for help.

When you are out on the trail a rider in front of you may start having trouble particularly if their horse is easily spooked. If this happens, stop, and wait until the other rider has things under control. Alternatively, you may want to check with the rider and see whether they would like you to take the lead as this may help to calm the frightened horse. As horses take cues from others, you may find that your horse suddenly decides that it does not want to go past what spooked the other horse, if this is the case stay back and wait until all of the horses have calmed down, and then move on.

Time for Games

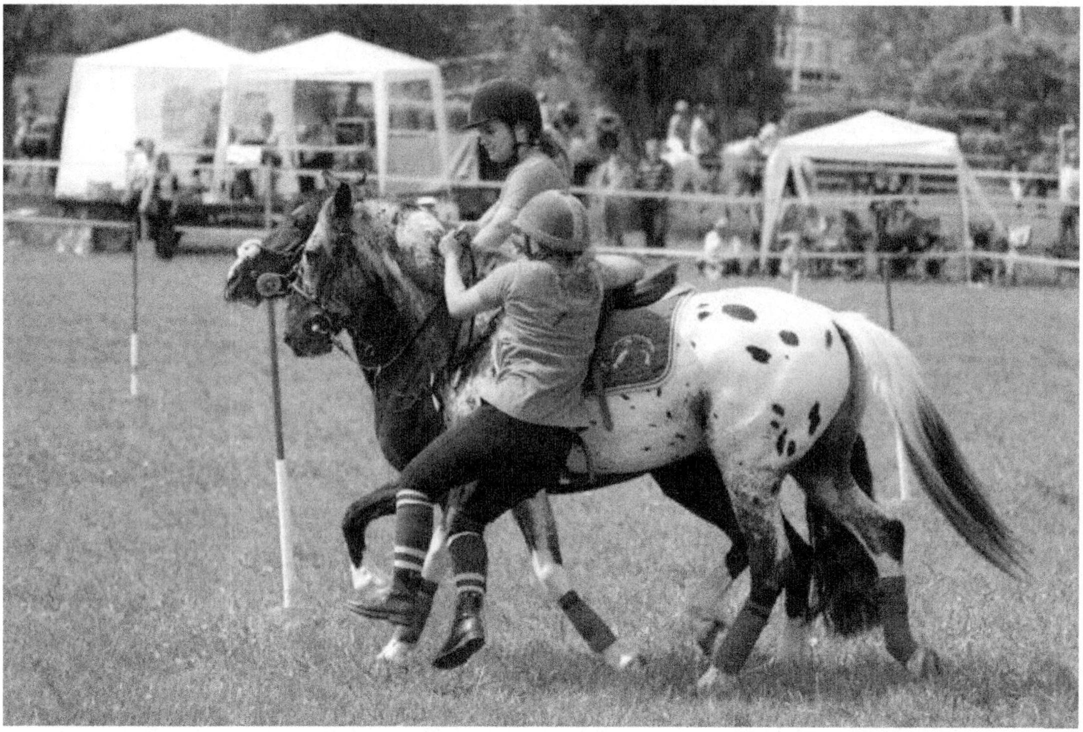

Playing games on horseback is a great way to help you develop good riding skills and relationships with your horse and also a perfect way to break the strict regime of riding lessons. They are a good deal of fun, too, for both you and your horse.

The games in this chapter are all suitable for beginners but should still only be played under the supervision of an instructor until you are more advanced. Safety is the number one concern when playing games on horseback, and all participants must be wearing an approved helmet.

Simon Says

In the arena, Simon Says helps riders to stretch their legs and also work on their balance. This game increases the rider's confidence in the saddle by proving that you can do more than one thing on a horse without falling off!

Simon Says on horseback is very similar to the version that is played on the ground. Everyone walks single file against the rail. The instructor periodically calls out different gaits or asks for specific maneuvers, such as turning a circle. The riders have to follow all of the instructor's instructions with the words "Simon Says". If the rider fails to perform the correct action, they are eliminated, the game continues until one rider remains, and they are then the winner.

Magazine Race

The Magazine Race is an arena relay race to see who can follow the instructions the best whilst getting on and off their horse. Teams can be formed with as many riders as the instructor chooses; however, the teams should all have the same number of participants. The instructor will place a pile of magazines on the ground at the end of the arena, and the riders line up at the other end. The instructor then gives each rider a page number, along with directions on how they have to hold the paper, such as in their teeth, under their seat, and so on, and which gait they should use.

Once the game starts, the first rider from each team rides to the end of the arena, gets off their horse, tears out the correct page number, gets back on their horse, and carry the paper back to their team at the other end; if the rider drops their paper they have to get off of their horse, pick it up, get back on and return to the line. The first team to have all of their riders finish the task are the winners.

Red Light, Green Light

Red light, Green light on horseback helps riders figure out how to stop and start their horses effectively and ride in a straight line.

Riders line up at one end of the arena at a start line, whilst the instructor draws the line at the other end of the arena. The instructor then faces the riders and says, "Green light" to get the riders moving; a few seconds later, the instructor says, "Red light", and the riders have to stop within 3 seconds, and if they fail to do this, they have to return to the start again. The game continues until one rider crosses the finish line. This game is usually played at a walk (maybe the occasional trot), depending on the riders' experience.

Ride-a-Buck

This popular horseback game is often played bareback and is an excellent way to teach riders good balance at various gaits. Riders line up at one end of the arena in single file. The instructor then puts a dollar bill under each rider's leg, elbow, calf, or seat, sticking out half of the bill. Riders then perform a variety of maneuvers and gaits that the instructor calls out. The last rider with the dollar bill in place is the winner.

Treasure Trail

This is a version of a Treasure Hunt that takes place on the trail. This is a good way for riders to develop their balance, mounting, and dismounting skills and the art of stopping and starting their horse.

The riders create teams (usually there are two people to a team), and each rider is given a list of things that they can find on the trail; these items can include things such as twigs, a flower, and so on. The riders have to stay in their teams for safety and collect the items within a time limit. Whichever team returns first with all or most of the items on the list is the winner.

Ride and Tie

Ride and Tie is a fun activity for both rider and instructor. Ride and Tie are also a recognized sport governed nationally by the Ride and Tie Association, and the event is also a lot of fun instructors can organize for their students. It helps beginners practice getting on and off their horses quickly and developing their skills in tying their horse up safely.

Traditional Ride and Tie events are made up of teams of three, two humans, and a horse. All three start on a trail simultaneously, with the horse and one mounted team member going on ahead. The track needs to be well marked and include places where it is safe to tie a horse up. When the rider gets to a point where they can safely tie up the horse, they stop and tie the horse up and then proceed on foot.

The team member that began on foot finds the tied-up horse, mounts, and continues past the other team member. They eventually stop, tie the horse back up, and walk on while the person they have passed catches up and gets on the horse again. This relay continues until all three of the team members have crossed the finish line. The winners are the team that finishes in the shortest amount of time.

Conclusion

Riding is challenging, exhilarating, demanding, rewarding, but also a great deal of fun. But, like any type of sport, you need to put in the time and effort so that you can participate effectively and safely.

One of the greatest passions in my life is horses and I do hope you will be as passionate about them now too and make horseback riding a regular part of your daily routine. I hope this book has provided you with the initial knowledge that you can build upon and become an excellent and accomplished horseman or horsewoman.

It is vital that you remember that no two horses are the same, some may get over their fears easily, whilst others need a lot of time and persuasion. Acting as if you have all the time in the world to sort out any issues rather than sticking to a strict regime and resolutions will come far sooner than you may first believe. The key here is patience. Open your heart to these spectacular animals and your life will never be dull again.

Printed in Great Britain
by Amazon